A Mirage Will Never Quench Your Thirst

A Source of Wisdom About Drugs

Compiled & Edited by
Laurent Weichberger
with Laura Smith

2003

SHERIAR FOUNDATION

© 2003 Laurent Weichberger

All of Meher Baba's words and messages quoted from *Lord Meher*, and *Love Alone Prevails*, are copyright © of Avatar Meher Baba Perpetual Public Charitable Trust, Kings Road, Ahmednagar, M.S., 414001 India.
USED BY PERMISSION

Quotes from *Lord Meher* Biography
copyright © Lawrence Reiter
USED BY PERMISSION

Quotes from *God in a Pill?* and *Life At Its Best*
copyright © Sufism Reoriented
USED BY PERMISSION

Cover photo of Meher Baba, Meherabad, India, 1937.

ISBN 1-88061927-X

No part of this book may be reproduced, stored in a retrieval system, or transmitted in any form or by any means, electronic, mechanical, photocopy, recording, or otherwise without prior written permission of the publisher, except by a reviewer who wishes to quote brief passages in connection with a review written for inclusion in a magazine, newspaper, or broadcast. For information write: Sheriar Foundation, 807 34th Ave. S., North Myrtle Beach, South Carolina 29582, USA, or visit www.sheriarbooks.org

Contents

Foreword	*v*
Preface	*xvii*
Introduction	*xxv*

1. Maladies of the Spirit	1
2. The Awakener	8
3. The Real and the False	28
4. Daily Attractions	37
5. Life Is Worth Living	44
6. Divine Intoxication	59
7. Voices of Experience	62
8. Meher Baba: The Highest of the High	95

God in a Pill? Revisited	*100*
Where to Get More Information	*112*
Glossary	*117*
Notes	*127*
Acknowledgements	*138*

FOREWORD

IN THE MID-1960S, three young men found their lives uniquely intertwined by the convergence of several factors: for one thing, each was a college or university student in the Cambridge/Boston area; for another, each, through various paths, was actively seeking spiritual reality. And all three were experimenting with drugs, from marijuana to LSD. They had met variously at meetings devoted to one spiritual quest or another, or through a mutual friend who was an assistant professor at Harvard and who smoked marijuana.

Then their world changed. Within a span of a few months, each came to know about Avatar Meher Baba, a spiritual master in India who declared himself to be the God-Man, the Christ of the Age – and whose message of truth, and life of love and compassion, gave credence to that claim.

Through acquaintance with Meher Baba came an exposure to his views on drugs, and soon these three – Allan Cohen, Robert Dreyfuss, and Rick Chapman – were working together to spread Baba's message. In the course of the several years that began after contact with Meher Baba, and spanned his passing in 1969 well into the early 1970s, these young men in particular had many opportunities to speak across the United States and in Europe about Meher Baba's drug message, and they became widely identified with that work. Now each one of these men again has an opportunity to speak about Meher Baba's drug message, in the form of a short foreword to this book.

RICK CHAPMAN

The simple fact that Laurent Weichberger has been inspired to bring together and publish this comprehensive account of Meher Baba's statements concerning drug use speaks volumes in itself: the urge to create this book and to make its message available to the public today bears testimony to the great and urgent need for it, as much now as when Meher Baba first made his definitive views about drug use public.

In the mid-to-late 1960s, psychedelic drugs were big news, and with them, the widespread use of pot was often taken as a natural concomitant to the psychedelic notion that drugs could help bring about a state of peace, joy, and enlightenment. Many who used such drugs then, in an effort to find spirituality or simply to find excitement or release, were astonished to discover that Meher Baba, considered by many seekers from various backgrounds to be the foremost spiritual authority of the time, opposed such experimentation. Or, to be more accurate, he was quick to put it into perspective, suggesting that those who had chanced upon spiritual realities while using drugs should quit while they were ahead, owing to the insidious nature of all such drug use to create more bindings, and eventual suffering, rather than the freedom and happiness many sought.

Although Meher Baba specifically named only a few drugs in the course of making many statements about drugs, he was very clear about what he meant. He declared that any drug taken "for what one could get out of it" could prove "harmful physically, mentally, and spiritually," and that such indulgence in drugs that had not been prescribed by a medical doctor solely for the purpose of improving one's health was misguided and wrong-headed. The spirit behind his warnings was, and remains, clear and direct: the attraction of any drug - from pot to acid, from speed to ecstasy, from sniffing glue to ... well, you name it – is like the call of the ancient Sirens when used without medical justification and prescription: beyond the allure of the altered states of mind such indulgence holds lie the inevitable rocks beneath the water, the great potential for becoming psychologically and spiritually shipwrecked. Meher Baba was as clear about this as he was about a nearly equally controversial perspective, namely, that the medical use of drugs like LSD is not only legitimate but can be effective in treating conditions ranging from alcoholism to schizophrenia.

I have witnessed many passionate arguments over Meher Baba's messages about drugs, and particularly about interpretations of which drugs they include and which they don't. If it weren't so serious a subject, it would all be very humorous, because, of course, the users of one drug or another tend vehemently to defend their drug of choice. But Meher Baba's warnings were probably not meant for those who are secure in their own self-knowledge and who are determined to pursue their desires in spite of his guidance; more likely, they were meant for seekers who know that they do not know everything and who might value illumination on the subject from one who knows and whose sole interest is our true well-being, happiness, and spiritual growth. See for yourself, in the same spirit in which Meher Baba so lovingly offered his guidance in response to the phenomenon of drug use in the 1960s.

ROBERT DREYFUSS

In 1965, I had the great good fortune of meeting Meher Baba in India. I had just hitchhiked across the world with the intention of confirming whether he could indeed be the One whom he asserted he was, the Avatar, God in human form. Being with him convinced me totally that he could be no one else.

At that time, Baba had not yet made any

statements regarding drug use. I had experimented with LSD and other substances as a way of sorting through the maze in an attempt to apprehend the Real. I was struck by the futility of this approach, as it did not last and was not complete. During my meeting with him, he clarified that drug use was "delusion within illusion," and that "if God can be found in a pill, then God is not worthy of being God." He asserted, "No drugs." From this meeting flowed much information about drug use and abuse, with great clarity. He emphasized that spreading his message about drugs was the most important spiritual work of the time.

His messages point to the futility of trying to escape from the very conditions generated through circumstances pertinent to each individual, created specifically to help one wake up from the addiction to illusion. He helps one to, however hesitantly, begin to take the path of sanity by awakening deeper values based in Reality.

He helps each individual to mirror a growing state of maturity so that the focus gradually shifts from oneself to the service of others.

Putting away the playthings of illusion is a necessary prelude to becoming who one truly is. The wisdom of no escape is integral to this process. May those who read this open their hearts to Meher Baba's unbounded love. This will lead to true healing of mind, body, and spirit.

ALLAN Y. COHEN

This book is a rich compilation of wise counsel and authoritative opinion on the relationship of psychoactive chemicals to human health, learning, and spiritual development.

Many communications from Meher Baba illuminate these issues. I personally received one of the first.

It was a sunny, fresh autumn day in 1964. I was a graduate student at Harvard, where I had come into contact with Timothy Leary and

Richard Alpert and quickly became absorbed in their extracurricular explorations of "better living through chemistry." The chemicals in question were psychedelic drugs. Learning of Meher Baba, the foremost living spiritual teacher in India, and finding that his clear and precise descriptions of higher consciousness seemed to parallel my own drug experiences, I had written him, never expecting an answer.

With great excitement, I tore open my first letter from India. I was stunned when I read its message, prepared by Adi K. Irani at Meher Baba's direction. Instead of validating my LSD-induced "elevation" of consciousness, Meher Baba emphatically stated that no drug of any kind could generate spiritual illumination. In this and subsequent letters, he clarified the folly of believing that drugs could be used as a path to God or enlightenment. With drugs, he explained, consciousness could be altered – for a time – but not truly raised or illumined.

Meher Baba drew a powerful and decisive contrast between authentic spiritual experience and the deceptive illusions created by chemical approaches to inner development. Gently but firmly, he indicated that the drug experiences I (and others) had described were as close to true spiritual experience as a mirage was to water: they appeared to be real, but nothing about them could ever really quench one's thirst for truth. At first I was taken aback – what, no shortcuts? No God-realization pill? Ultimately, however, I came to understand Meher Baba's statements on drugs as loving reminders of the difference between Illusion and Reality.

Meher Baba's description of the limitations of "mind-altering" drugs was unerringly precise. His review of the physical, psychological, and spiritual consequences of their use has been strongly supported by later scientific research. After nearly four decades of professional work in the substance abuse field, I find that Meher

Baha's central principles about drugs remain relevant and contemporary:

(1) The drug experience is always temporary;
(2) Even with the best of drug experiences, individuals gain only a distorted perception of the lower levels of the inner life; that is entirely different in nature from the experience of true spiritual advancement; and
(3) Long-term nonmedical drug involvement, leading inevitably to psychological imbalance or chemical dependency, is an unnecessary waste of vast human potential.

Meher Baba advised spiritual seekers and youth to avoid a wide range of psychoactive and addictive substances. Yet he recognized and even specified legitimate medical uses for such drugs. And with his encompassing love and wisdom, he made it very clear that from a spiritual point of view, those who experiment with drugs and those who become caught in the cycle of dependency and addiction to drugs and/or alcohol are not evil, nor are they denied God's compassion and help.

I was one of many who were lucky enough to hear Meher Baba's wake-up call about drugs and spirituality. Some of us, including other contributors to this book, were asked by Meher Baba to spread his messages about drugs to the general public through lectures and seminars, in articles and interviews, and even on radio and television. More often than we expected, we were privileged to see how these clear and cogent statements of simple truth opened minds and hearts not only to Divine Wisdom but also to Divine Love.

PREFACE

SOMETIME IN THE 1920S, Meher Baba wrote a ghazal that contained the following lines:

> Do not take forbidden intoxicants,
> better to live a life of honor and esteem.
>
> Learn to live in the unique intoxication
> of the early morning love of God.[1]

I first read this poem in 1987, when the first volume of *Lord Meher*, the multi-volume biography of Meher Baba, was published. I now had access to many previously unavailable words from my Spiritual Master, Meher Baba, and drank deeply all that he was sharing so many years ago.

Since then I have had many experiences that have brought home the importance of his message against the use of drugs. It was not until the 1990s that I became acutely aware of the seriousness of the drug problem in America, and even more alarming to me, drug abuse among spiritual seekers.

I remember how the idea of creating this book all started. One day in the early 1990s someone gave me a copy of the Buddhist magazine *Tricycle*, and this particular issue was dedicated to drug use and "enlightenment." Knowing what Meher Baba had stated about the physical, mental, and spiritual dangers of drug abuse, I was horrified at what I discovered within those pages. Not only were many spiritually minded people experimenting with drug use in relation to their desire for enlightenment, but one article was seriously asking the question whether one could be considered a true Buddhist without using drugs! In any case, at the end of the magazine they published a long directory of contact information for many Buddhist centers in America.

Suddenly, I felt overwhelmed by an urge to acquire as many copies as possible of a 1966 pamphlet entitled *God in a Pill?: Meher Baba on L.S.D. and the High Roads*, which contained Meher Baba's many statements about drugs. I planned to write a cover letter stating that Meher Baba was emphatic that drug use would not help the seeker to reach enlightenment, and send it with a copy of *God in a Pill?* to every Buddhist center listed in the magazine. So I went to Sheriar Books in Myrtle Beach, South Carolina. I tried to buy as many copies as I could from Ann Conlon, who was working in the bookstore that day. She asked me why I wanted so many, so I told her my story. She remarked that the old 1966 drug pamphlet was really getting quite dated and needed to be redone for a more modern audience. Surprisingly, she then asked me if I would be willing to do this work.

Not expecting such a question, I became puzzled. I recall that something inside clearly told me, "Yes," but I really didn't feel qualified. The conversation continued until finally I said that I would at least try.

Then in 1994, the Atlanta Meher Baba group sponsored a special series of lectures on the entire life of Meher Baba, in celebration of his 100th birthday. The plan was to deliver twelve speeches on Meher Baba's life, each one to cover a portion of his lifetime. I volunteered, and chose to speak on the last years of his life, from 1966 to 1969. I was very fortunate that Lawrence (Hermes) Reiter, the publisher of *Lord Meher*, allowed me to read the manuscript draft which covered those years, and I learned a lot about what Baba was saying and doing toward the end of his life. Amazingly to me, Baba had put a tremendous amount of energy and effort toward educating people about the harmful effects of drugs, especially warning them against the use of LSD. It was as a direct result of doing the research for that talk that I acquired the courage to approach this project.

But still I felt very insecure and unworthy to undertake the drug work for Baba. By a strange twist of fate, I found myself living in Arizona with my wife and daughter, and was suddenly unemployed. I looked in the local newspaper's help-wanted section and found a job at a drug-testing laboratory. I literally arranged for drug testing nationwide, and had to learn all about various drugs, how they affect the nervous system, and much more. At this point, I started to feel that Baba had arranged this so that I could feel strong enough to begin writing for this project. But the nagging thought kept popping up: what about Rick Chapman, Robert Dreyfuss, and Allan Cohen? How would they feel about my trying to work on this?

So, it was not until I contacted Allan, Rick, and Robert and received their overwhelmingly positive encouragement and support that I felt totally committed. Don Stevens has also been very instrumental, especially in the last stages of production, in providing much-needed encouragement.

This book is offered to those who have used drugs (taken to alter consciousness) or are thinking about using such drugs, and are interested in spirituality or in simply living a healthier life. As humanity proceeds into the next millennium, we can look back historically on the challenges that have we have encountered here in America as well as globally. There is little doubt that one of the most severe challenges facing our global culture today is that of drug abuse. The goal in creating this book has been to offer a holistic aid, among many needed, to help those individuals who wish to break free from the seduction of intoxicants once and for all.

I have included a section entitled "Voices of Experience" in which those who have had direct contact with drug use share their experiences, which speak for themselves. Also provided are two appendices: *"God in a Pill? Revisited,"* which reprints a complete and sequential record of all the sayings about drugs by Meher Baba in that pamphlet, and "Where to Get More Information," for those interested in further reading and other resources such as web sites.

Meher Baba did not speak for the last forty-four years of his life, using various methods to communicate in silence.[2] Considering the nature of interpretation, it is very important to read Meher Baba's words in the context in which they were given. For this purpose I have provided source information for each quote (whenever possible) in the Notes at the end of the book.

Baba once said in regard to work, "...Leave

the fruit of action to Me or to God."[3] Beloved Meher, to you I now leave the fruits of this work. May it please you.

— *L.W.*

INTRODUCTION

THROUGHOUT HISTORY, individuals have publicly spoken out for or against a variety of issues, acting as a public conscience of the masses. While people have come to expect this type of behavior from politicians, celebrities, and the like, many have a deep distrust of their words, which may stem from political motives or self-interest. However, there are always those rare individuals whose motives are pure and who work selflessly to uplift humanity. Whether these special people come to be looked upon as saints or sages, humanitarians, or just good people, time has continually honored their words above and beyond those of their contemporaries.

Meher Baba is such a person, one who has

shared his unique perspective from the depths of his direct spiritual experience. Concerning drug use, Meher Baba sought to spread his message that drugs do not help in the search for Truth, but actually cause great harm and distract from the real spiritual path.

Meher Baba took his stand regarding drug use during the 1960s when many were using LSD and other drugs as a means to "expand consciousness" or find the Truth. He responded to this popular idea by firmly refuting it and stating, "To attempt to approach the Creator of universes and the Beloved of hearts through drugs is to mock the majesty of God and insult your own intelligence." [4]

Drug users today are more apt to describe themselves as "recreational" users in search of fun and escape, or an emotional high such as experienced through the drug known as ecstasy. Although the reasons for drug use today may appear different than they were in the 1960s, the basic motives of self-forgetfulness, apparent freedom, and the desire for escape are the same. Meher Baba's message about drugs is just as important and valuable now as when it originated.

The inspiration for writing this book is that it may serve in some way as a bridge from one way of looking at life, and its many choices, to a healthier way that includes spiritual reality and its consequences. We dedicate this book with fervent hopes (and prayers) that even one person may find within these pages the spiritual guidance and insight needed to avoid drug use altogether. For those already using drugs, may you have the strength and courage to give them up in exchange for a real and lasting spiritual high.

Laurent Weichberger, Flagstaff, Ariz.
Laura Smith, Myrtle Beach, S.C.

I.

MALADIES OF THE SPIRIT

ONE DOES NOT HAVE TO BE interested in spirituality to realize the negative consequences of using drugs. Physically, the experiences of appetite changes, headaches, weight loss, and the general breakdown of the functioning of the body are common. As drugs are used more frequently the body generally becomes more tolerant of their presence in the system. Thus greater quantities of the drug are required in order to achieve the desired effect, dramatically increasing the danger of accidental overdose resulting in hospitalization or death. Mentally, memory loss, hallucinations, flashbacks, delusions, and paranoia can occur. And ultimately users cannot ignore the spiritual bankruptcy resulting from drug use.

On a more personal level, many drug users become isolated, uninterested in what life has to offer, and unable to function in society. They find it difficult to take good care of themselves and adequately discharge their responsibilities, resulting in the long-term lowering of self-esteem and depression.

So given all these dangers, why do people use drugs to begin with? There are the obvious reasons associated with "recreational" use, such as escape from the normal stresses of everyday life, the quest for pleasure, curiosity about exploring nonordinary levels of perception, or maybe just the desire to fit in socially. Some users may have experienced a great amount of physical or emotional hurt in their lives – and turn to drugs in an effort to numb the pain. People suffering from clinical depression or anxiety may "self-medicate" with illegal drugs instead of seeking medical care.

Does it work? As with many things, there are two sides to this coin. Drugs may deliver much of the initial promise to the user, as the circle of friends seem to increase, everyone seems to be having more fun, and the pains of yesterday are all but forgotten. The tragedy is that drug experiences are temporary: what goes up must come down.

Yet drug abuse is not the essential problem in itself, but rather a symptom of a much deeper and more profound problem. It is for this reason that a solution to drug abuse has often eluded professional psychotherapists and drug counselors. Unless a remedy can be found and applied to the root causes of drug abuse, we will never finish treating the symptoms.

One highly respected family therapist specializing in the treatment of addiction, Craig Nakken, in his book *The Addictive Personality*, gave this definition of addiction: "Addiction is an illness in which people believe in and seek spiritual connection through objects and behaviors that can only produce temporary sensations. These repeated, vain attempts to connect with the Divine produce hopelessness, fear, and grieving that further alienate the addict from spirituality and humanity."[5] Thus, it can be said that the basis of addiction lies in the anguish of separateness and the search for love and connection. If this is true, then both the malady and the cure are, in actuality, spiritual in nature.

Yet even the best-trained, most experienced psychoanalysts and drug counselors have not been able to determine the full spiritual consequences of drug abuse or find a real solution. Just as it is important to consult a doctor when concerned with medical issues, or a lawyer regarding legal problems, so it is wise to consult a spiritual authority on matters of the spirit.

Meher Baba speaks with spiritual authority when he says:

> Essentially, we are all one. I am greater than none of you in the soul-sense and really speaking, none of you have to receive divinity from Me, as that divinity is eternally existing equally in us all; but what I have to give is the knowledge and the experience of the oneness of all.[6]

Concerning drug use Meher Baba said:

> It is human, and therefore necessarily wrongsighted, to view the result of the drug by its immediate relative effects – to calculate its end result is beyond human knowledge, and only the true Guide can point the way.[7]

One of the hallmarks of Meher Baba's communication is that while he shed much light on the consequences of certain actions, throughout his life he rarely gave absolute rules about what "to do" or what "not to do." As he said, "I have come not to teach but to awaken. Understand therefore that I lay down no precepts."[8]

An exception to this pattern occurred in the late 1960s, when drug use in America, and throughout the world, was increasing significantly. When it had reached unprecedented levels, Meher Baba gave his general admonishments against drug use. He even went so far as to say, "No drugs." Of course, we know that Baba was referring not to appropriately prescribed remedies but (in particular) to hallucinogens such as LSD. He declared:

> Any drug when used medically for diseases, under the direct supervision of a medical practitioner, is not impermissible and cannot be classified with individual usage of a drug for what one can get out of it – or hope to get out of it – whether thrills, forgetfulness, or a delusion of spiritual experience.[9]

Meher Baba was a man whose life itself inspired countless souls to give up unhealthy ways of living, including drug abuse, in favor of more disciplined mental control and ever increasing love for God. For individuals striving to live a more spiritual life, Meher Baba has promised to help them spiritually, to guide them in knowing their real Self.

Most of what Meher Baba said regarding drug use took place within the context of the 1960s. Although society has changed and the motivations for drug use today may be different, Meher Baba's words continue to shed light for those seeking truth and genuine spiritual guidance.

2.
THE AWAKENER

MEHER BABA HAD BECOME a very popular Spiritual Master during the 1960s just as LSD use was running rampant in America. At that time many people were drawn to the use of drugs, particularly hallucinogens, with the aim of discovering the meaning of life, experiencing cosmic consciousness and achieving enlightenment. Through the use of LSD, people claimed to have great spiritual insights. It is understandable therefore, that people using LSD with spiritual motivations looked to Baba for guidance, and as always, he was there for them, sharing from the depth of his knowledge.

In 1964, Allan Y. Cohen, then a Harvard graduate student, had started using LSD in the hopes of "attaining spiritual freedom" and was inspired to share his LSD experiences with Kitty Davy, one of Baba's disciples at the Meher Spiritual Center in Myrtle Beach, South Carolina. Kitty contacted Baba in India to bring this to his attention, and he responded to Allan directly with these words:

> All so-called spiritual experiences generated by taking "mind-changing" drugs such as LSD, mescaline and psilocybin are superficial and add enormously to one's addiction to the deceptions of illusion which is but the shadow of Reality.
>
> The experience of a semblance of freedom that these drugs may temporarily give to one is in actuality a millstone round the aspirant's neck in his efforts toward emancipation from the rounds of birth and death!
>
> But there is no drug that can promote

the aspirant's progress – nor ever alleviate the sufferings of separation from his beloved God. LOVE is the only propeller and the only remedy. The aspirant should love God with all his heart till he forgets himself and recognizes his beloved God in himself and others. [10]

In 1965 Meher Baba instructed one of his Mandali, Eruch Jessawala, to write a letter to the brothers Irwin and Edward Luck, in which he said, "Experiences induced through drugs like LSD are nothing short of spiritual hallucinations, and if God could be experienced through drugs and [hemp] cigarettes, God is not worthy of being God!"[11]

Although Meher Baba lived in India, he was intensely concerned with the future of America. He gave specific instructions to three of his American followers – Allan Cohen, Rick Chapman, and Robert Dreyfuss – for spreading his message about drug use. During Robert's visit to Meher

Baba in India on November 17, 1965, Baba asked him whether many young people in America were taking drugs. Robert replied that they were. Baba then stated:

> Tell those that are, that if drugs could make one realize God, then God is not worthy of being God.
>
> No drugs.
>
> Many people in India smoke hashish and ganja. They see colors and forms and lights, and it makes them elated. But this elation is only temporary. It is a false experience. It gives only experience of illusion, and serves to take one farther away from reality...
>
> Tell those who indulge in these drugs (LSD, etc.) that it is harmful physically, mentally, and spiritually, and that they should stop taking these drugs. Your duty is to tell them, regardless of whether they accept what you say, or if they ridicule or

> humiliate you, to boldly and bravely face these things. Leave the results to me. I will help you in my work...
>
> You are to bring my message to those ensnared in the drug-net of illusion, that they should abstain, that the drugs will bring more harm than good. I send my love to them.[12]

At another time, Baba said to Robert:

> Go back to the U.S.A. – spread My love among others, particularly among the young, and persuade them to desist from taking drugs, for they are harmful physically – mentally – spiritually.[13]

Dreyfuss, Cohen, and Chapman subsequently offered public talks about Meher Baba's message against drugs at universities and colleges around America and also in Europe.

Others also had direct interactions with Baba concerning the topic of drugs. On April 21,

1966, Meher Baba instructed his secretary, Adi K. Irani, to write Ivy Duce, who was then the Murshida (or teacher) of Sufism Reoriented in America. His letter responded to a *New York Times* article about American students and drugs, which was read to Baba. The letter says:

> A special article in *The New York Times* by Robert B. Semple, Jr., on "Colleges Warned to Curb Drug Use – U.S. Asserts Hallucinogens May Harm Students" was read to Beloved Baba in Poona.
>
> After hearing the article, Baba wishes me to let you and those concerned know that if the student world continues to indulge in the use of LSD, half of the U.S.A. would soon become mentally deranged! Hence, a check must be strictly enforced, and the use of these drugs be prohibited, especially amongst the rising generation.

The letter continued:

> Baba wishes Robert Dreyfuss, Allan Cohen, Rick Chapman and others who have stopped taking LSD and such drugs, to be his apostles in this particular field. ...[14]

The year 1966 was to yield many clarifications from Baba regarding drugs, as correspondence flew back and forth between America and India.

In response to pressing questions from Allan Cohen and others, Baba clarified his statements on July 14, 1966, through Adi:

> 1. Meher Baba did say that the user of LSD could never reach subtle consciousness[15] in this incarnation despite its repeated use, unless the person surrendered to a Perfect Master.[16] To experience real, spiritual consciousness, surrenderance to a Perfect Master is necessary.

2. The experiences gained through LSD are, in some cases, experiences of the shadows of the subtle plane in the gross world. These experiences have nothing at all to do with spiritual advancement.

3. Beloved Baba stresses that repeated use of LSD leads to insanity which may prove incurable in mental cases, even with LSD treatment.

4. Medical use of LSD helps to cure, in some cases, mental disorders and madness.

5. There is no such thing as "areas in the brain reserved for subtle consciousness," and the question of LSD affecting them has no meaning.

6. When LSD is used for genuine medical purposes, in controlled doses under the supervision of specialists, there are no chances of the brain, liver or kidney being damaged.

> 7. Baba answered again that continued LSD use for non-medical purposes results in madness, and eventually death."[17]

A married couple, Mik Hamilton and Ursula Reinhart, visited Baba at Meherazad, India in 1966. Mik had a profound and natural conviction in Meher Baba's spiritual status and wanted to obey Baba, who advised the couple, *"God Speaks* and *Stay with God* are the two most important books to read." Then he continued, "Go to America and dissuade young people from taking drugs. Encourage, persuade them to stop taking drugs. To do that is the highest spiritual work to be done in the world today."[18]

The use of LSD had spread like wildfire across America and the entire Western world. Even long-time disciples of genuine God-realized Masters, in their quest for spiritual experiences, contemplated using LSD, and in some cases did use LSD because of the hype surrounding it. In response to this, knowing exactly how serious the situation really was, Meher Baba said, "This craze will die its natural death."[19]

Eruch Jessawala was firmly reprimanded by Baba after speaking lightly about the use of LSD. As described in *Lord Meher* by Bhau Kalchuri:

> When the subject of LSD had first arisen, Dr. Goher obtained a medical book describing how LSD had been used to treat mental patients. It was legal at the time and could be prescribed by a physician. Eruch, being interested in such things, was reading the book one day when Baba came along. He asked what he was reading and Eruch said, "It is a medical book which describes the effects of the LSD drug." Teasingly, Eruch added, "Kirpal Singh told us we should have experiences. Since you don't give us any, I am thinking of taking this LSD." Then finished – "We can get experiences!"

Baba was rather upset by his sarcastic comments and told him to put the book away. "Why are you reading such rubbish?" he asked. "Don't ever think of ingesting it!"[20]

Another follower of Meher Baba, Don Stevens,[21] received a similar reprimand from the Master. Bhau Kalchuri writes:

> Because Don Stevens was involved with the Sufi Center [Sufism Reoriented] in San Francisco to which many young people were now coming, Baba sent him copies of the correspondence about LSD and other drugs between himself, Allan Cohen, Robert Dreyfuss and Richard Alpert, which he wished put together into a pamphlet called *God in a Pill?*.[22]
>
> Don Stevens was not particularly interested in the subject of drugs, and joked, "You know, Baba, I seem to be get-

ting more and more entangled into these young people's lives. So many of them have had drug experiences that have been terribly important to them. I think in order to know more[23] about this subject, I'm going to have to try one LSD trip myself!"

Baba, as soon as Stevens said this, reared back in his seat, bristled and lightning flashed from his eyes. In a warning tone[24] he stated, "Don, don't even think of such a thing! You do not understand the sort of consequences this can have on the individual's nervous system."

Baba continued, "It is true that one individual may take one hundred or even two hundred doses of LSD without any permanent, substantial damage to his nervous system; however, for another person of a different temperament, of a different nervous system setup, just one dose can be absolutely, permanently, irretrievably harmful. So, don't even think in jest of such a thing!"

Don Stevens has directly clarified[25] what happened next:

> Baba entered into some minutes of interchange with Eruch on what was obviously a point that was both important and also difficult to render into the proper words. I mention this, as it was the second major occasion on which Baba spent quite some minutes in my presence trying to arrive with Eruch at a completely satisfying expression, and finally Eruch had to say that as close as he could come to what Baba was trying to convey, was the following:
>
> "Baba is trying to express the danger of what is being attempted through the use of LSD to open certain psychic centers,

but the closest I can arrive to his meaning is to compare this with someone who owns a fine Swiss watch, and who is trying to get inside it and open it up, and the instrument he is using is a crowbar."

And that was not a volunteered statement from Eruch, but Eruch's effort to put into words what Baba had been explaining to Eruch to explain to me. Eruch left the problem there, and frankly, I had no trouble in seeing what Baba was trying to get over to me.

Bhau writes about this exchange between Baba, Eruch, and Don: "Baba stated even this analogy did not quite give the true picture, or take into account the enormous risk a person was taking with such powerful drugs."[26]

Then, in 1967, a well-known Dutch film director, Louis van Gasteren, interviewed Meher Baba at Meherazad, his home in India, while a cameraman shot the footage. The film was finally released in 1997, and the following words were transcribed from Meher Baba's gestured replies to Louis as interpreted by Eruch:[27]

> Now in India, since ages, there are those who have been used to drugs – they are drug addicts. They are the ones who take ganja, then they take charas, and bhang – and they feel uplifted when they take these drugs. And they see colors and signs, and they feel, through their hallucinations, that they have reached the goal.
>
> And that false experience is also not continuous. There is a break in their experience. And that is the reason why it is not real.
>
> Those who take ganja and drugs, they get uplifted through the drugs, and then, in the end, they go crazy – mad...
>
> Now we come to those persons who have experiences through drugs. They

> feel that they have realized God because they get certain experiences. But the guideline is it is not continuous. Even though that is hallucination, even that is not continuous. And that is the sign that it is not true experience. Such experiences are harmful physically, mentally, and spiritually.
>
> And when I break my Silence,[28] I say that the world will come to know what God is – God is because you are. You are because God is. But that experience, one in a million can have.

It is interesting to note that Baba did not state that LSD should never be used. He clearly states that it can be used medically as a cure, "in some cases." To help put Baba's statements in context, consider how a physician uses a certain drug, versus how an individual may abuse the same drug. For example, we know that an emergency room doctor at a hospital will administer morphine, a powerful opiate, to a patient who is suffering great pain, so that a medical procedure may be performed to save the patient's life. If morphine is taken by an individual for the pain-killing effects without medical supervision, the result may lead to an overdose. In the same way, LSD can be used for rare medical conditions, but abuse of LSD can lead to madness or even death. As Baba explained:

> Medically there are legitimate uses of LSD. It can be used beneficially for chronic alcoholism, for severe and serious cases of depression and for relief in mental illnesses. Use of LSD other than for specific medical purposes is *harmful* physically, mentally and spiritually.

> LSD and other psychedelic drugs should never be used except when prescribed by a professional medical practitioner in the case of serious mental disorder under his direct supervision.

- Proper use of LSD under direct supervision of a medical practitioner could help to cure insanity. It could lead to insanity if used for purposes other than strictly medical.[29]

- Use of LSD produces hallucinations, and prolonged use of this drug will lead to mental derangement, which even the medical use of LSD would fail to cure.

- In short, LSD can be used beneficially for specific medical purposes, but for spiritual progress it is not only useless but positively harmful.[30]

In order to impress the reality of the dangers involved in drug abuse, specifically the use of LSD, Meher Baba had launched a campaign against ignorance. By spreading his in-depth message against drug abuse he effectively revealed what is at stake for the individual drug user's body, mind and spirit, as well as the fine points of the spiritual path to enlightenment. While many saw LSD as a short-cut to spiritual experience or enlightenment, Baba was quick to point out the error of their ways when he said,

> LSD is absolutely of no use for any kind of spiritual awakening.[31]

> Taking LSD is harmful physically, mentally and spiritually. But if you take me into your heart and love me as your real Self, you will find me in you as the Infinite Ocean of Effulgence. And this experience will remain continuously throughout eternity.[32]

When Rick Chapman visited Meherazad in June 1966, Baba asked his Australian poet-disciple Francis Brabazon to recite one of his poems for Rick. It contained this couplet:

> Don't try to hold me up by offering me a trip on LSD;
>
> I always travel unencumbered, guided alone by love – see![33]

In addition to LSD, Meher Baba gave a short but candid description of the consequences of using opiates (such as opium, heroin, and morphine).

> One who is addicted to opium (eating or smoking) derives a... feeling of well-being, though temporarily. After a time the opium addict begins to feel the after-effects of opium in severe constipation, loss of appetite, headache, dullness and drowsiness. He then begins to realize that it would have been better had he not become addicted. But unfortunately, he cannot give up the habit. He has become a slave. He realizes this too late, and sinks into deeper addiction, being tempted to take greater and greater quantities of opium to keep pace with the gradual loss of the feeling of well-being.[34]

3.
THE REAL AND THE FALSE

ALTHOUGH THE PARTICULAR CRAZE of searching for Truth through drugs seems to have died for the most part, various other drug crazes continue to pop up. Nevertheless, the spiritual consequences of drug use remain, along with the harmful physical and mental effects. Meher Baba discloses the true measure of spiritual experience versus experience gained through drug use:

- Just as it is difficult to distinguish an imitation from a real pearl, so it is difficult to distinguish between an imitation and a real spiritual experience. Once gained, the real experience is never lost; it is permanent.[35]

- All the experiences even of spiritual aspirants on the Path to God-realization (gotten in the natural course of involution of consciousness) are of the domain of Illusion and are ephemeral and absolutely unimportant; how much more illusory and distracting are the experiences through substances compounded in a laboratory which have the semblance of those of the aspirant on the Spiritual Path! The one and only true experience is the experience of the Truth, the Reality; for once the realization of God is attained it remains a continual and never-ending experience.

The all-pervading effulgence of God the Reality can only be experienced by an aspirant who keeps himself scrupulously above all illusory experimentations and humbly takes refuge in love of God. [36]

There is also a state of perverted consciousness. It is a state in which consciousness indulges in induced experiences such as those gotten from the use of drugs; and even the most fantastic experiences thus induced are only the shadows of the subtle plane experienced in the gross world.[37]

- It is absolutely essential for a spiritual aspirant who genuinely longs for union with God – the Reality – to shun experiments with the effects of certain drugs. These things do not uplift the aspirant nor draw him out of the rut of Illusion. Experiences born of these practices wear off as soon as the aspirant withdraws from or is thrown out of the orbit of the effect produced by the technique employed.[38]

- The experiences which drugs induce are as far removed from Reality as is a mirage from water. No matter how much you pursue the mirage you will never quench your thirst, and the search for Truth through drugs must end in disillusionment.[39]

> One who knows the Way, who is the Way, cannot approve of the continued pursuance of a method that not only must prove fruitless but leads away from the Path that leads to Reality.
>
> No drug, whatever its great promise, can help one to attain the spiritual goal. There is no short-cut to the goal except through the grace of the Perfect Master, and drugs, LSD more than others, give only a semblance of "spiritual experience," a glimpse of a false Reality.[40]

As a means of comparison, Meher Baba gives further explanations regarding various spiritual experiences not induced by drugs:

> An example of experiences that are shadows of the subtle plane encountered in the gross world is that of a yogi who taught his 150 students to go into trance. When the students came out of

the trance they were asked by the yogi to describe their experiences. Their accounts would be amazing to a man in the street, for in their state of trance they saw lights and colours galore–dazzling lights in colours and in circles and in different designs. They felt all things around them pulsating with life and felt themselves separate from their own bodies and become witness to all things. Even such experiences as these are but the shadows of the subtle plane experienced in the gross world, for they are not continuous. However, these are NOT spiritually harmful, but neither are they spiritually beneficial. But experiences induced through the use of drugs are harmful physically.

- Even actual experiences of the subtle planes in the subtle sphere (which are always continuous) are likened to the pleasure of children playing with toys. However, these experiences are spiritually beneficial since they create a longing in the aspirant for further advancement. But union with God is impossible without the grace of the Perfect Master.[41]

- Even the experiences of the planes of consciousness are only another kind of illusion! Experiences of the planes are "Real Illusion," whereas those derived from the use of drugs are illusion into "False illusion." This mundane life and the experiences thereof are a "dream into a dream"; whereas the traversing of the spiritual path by the seekers who gain experiences of planes of consciousness is a "dream."[42]

One important aspect of Meher Baba's vantage point is that it includes living Perfect Masters, meaning those people who continually experience union with God after having attained the consciousness of God-realization, and who continue to live the life of an enlightened Master of Wisdom. In various faiths these Perfect Masters are called by different names, including Sadguru, Qutub, and Man-God, but such a Master should be carefully distinguished from the spiritual status of a "saint" who is still longing for God, and striving to reach the goal of God-realization.

According to Meher Baba, the only spiritual experience that can be considered fully Real is that of God-realization. It is therefore beneficial to acquire even the smallest glimpse of what God-realization means. As Meher Baba has explained:

> God-realization is the very goal of all creation. All earthly pleasure, however great, is but a fleeting shadow of the eternal bliss of God-realization. All worldly knowledge, however comprehensive, is but a distorted reflection of the absolute

Truth of God-realization. All human might, however imposing, is but a fragment of the infinite power of God-realization. All that is noble, beautiful, and lovely, all that is great, good, and inspiring in the universe, is just an infinitesimal fraction of the unfading and unspeakable glory of God-realization.

The eternal bliss, the infinite power, the unfading glory, and the absolute Truth of God-realization are not to be had for nothing. The individualized soul has to go through all the travail, the pain, and the struggle of evolution, reincarnation, and involution before it can inherit this treasure, which is hidden at the heart of creation. The price it has to pay for coming into possession of this treasure is its own existence as a separate ego. The limited individuality must disappear entirely if there is to be an entrance into the unlimited state of Godhood.

In the ordinary person of the world, the limited individuality, which is identified with a finite name and form, predominates and creates a veil of ignorance over the God within. If this ignorance is to disappear, the limited individual has to surrender his own limited existence. When he goes from the scene without leaving a vestige of his limited life, what remains is God. The surrenderance of limited existence is the surrender of the firmly rooted delusion of having a separate existence. It is not the surrender of anything real: it is the surrenderance of the false and the inheritance of the Truth."[43]

4.

DAILY ATTRACTIONS

IN ADDITION TO DRUGS, Meher Baba also made statements concerning alcohol and other everyday addictions such as tobacco, coffee, and tea.

In the early 1930s when America was still struggling with the prohibition issue, Baba visited America and spent weeks in Hollywood, attending parties and receiving visitors wherever he stayed. He had many opportunities to share his unique point of view:

> There is no question but that those who drink habitually do so in order to experience release. They want something that will lift them out of their crystallization of thought and action, and free them, if,

only for the moment, for original expression. That the fact of this method of obtaining release may not be the best one does not concern them – they know no other as yet. If they could be made to realize that the liberation they seek could be more easily and more completely attained by the control of thought and desire, they would certainly practice that control instead of drinking. I will teach many how to free themselves from drink.[44]

Baba speaks eloquently here about the problem of alcohol:

> Recourse to alcohol for drowning one's sorrows is a perverted form of solace. Solace afforded by things outside of you is synonymous with doping, which gives a certain amount of relief or relaxation. Real and unalloyed solace is within you.[45]

Here again, we see how Baba continuously draws a distinction between false values and true values, gently nudging us away from the ways of the world, and toward the spiritual way of God:

- While wine leads to self-oblivion, Divine Love leads to self-knowledge.[46]

- Wine is prepared by the crushing and further crushing of grapes, when it acquires the capacity for intoxication, which usually takes away one's command of understanding. Close and repeated feeling of love for God also brings intoxication, but this takes you towards true understanding.[47]

- Wine is good for both health and the spiritual life. It is an intoxicant and tonic for both. If after drinking wine, thoughts are diverted to spiritual advancement, it is a great push toward the Goal; other-

> wise, it can lead to hell. Wine is such that either it raises you to the highest pinnacle or makes you fall into the deepest ditch.[48]

Baba again stresses the fact that intoxication gained by substances, including alcohol, is not continuous and therefore cannot lead to lasting happiness.

> Why does a man commit suicide? Because he expects to find happiness in death. Why does another man drink? It is because of the happiness he expects to derive from alcohol. But what happiness is derived, and how long does it last? So long as the effect of intoxication lasts. No sooner does it cool down than he feels broken, dejected and miserable.[49]

Regarding his own personal habits and those of his disciples, Baba said:

> Once in a great while I give wine to my lovers, and make them understand that it is not this wine of grapes, but the true wine of love, giving divine intoxication, that helps towards union with God.[50]

Meher Baba once compared alcohol, drugs, and tobacco:

> Alcoholic drinks in ordinary moderate doses act as stimulants and are harmless. If taken in excess they are harmful. Drugs, whether in small or large doses, are injurious. They have a characteristic of making the users addicts. Starting from small doses, and very subtly, they tempt the partakers to increase the quantity indiscriminately until they cannot do without them and become addicted.
>
> Tobacco and smoking has only the slight advantage of deriving superficial pleasure, which is temporary. But there

are three distinct disadvantages: physical, mental and habitual. Physically it spoils the system and mentally it tortures one when unavailable.[51]

Since many in the West can be fanatical about drinking coffee (and, more recently, drinking tea or "chai"), it may be helpful to include Baba's statements about these beverages as well.

- Tea or coffee, though injurious, is not so injurious as tobacco, alcohol, bhang-ganja, and other strong intoxicants. Rather these – tea or coffee – are in some cases beneficial, particularly when medically advised and taken in mild form. Excessive use of these, and in stronger forms, is as injurious as tobacco, alcohol, etc.[52]

- Strong tea provides a very good stimulant to tired nerves. But it causes no real improvement in health. On the contrary,

> Tea is a drink liked by most persons in all countries. In Gujarati we call it chaha, which also means love. Both these chahas, if confined within material limits, have no spiritual value. One chaha – tea – is injurious to health if taken in excess, and the other chaha – love – may be injurious to spiritual growth if it is for tea and sense-pleasures.[54]

the general health is usually undermined with strong stimulants.[53]

What does Baba mean by this last statement about the two loves (chahas)? In a lighthearted way, he is saying that in his native language of Gujarati the word for tea also means "love." So there are two types of love that have no spiritual value: love for tea and love for sensual objects of the world. Both of these loves keep one from spiritual growth.

5.
LIFE IS WORTH LIVING

FOR THOSE WHO HAVE STRUGGLED with addiction or the temptation to experiment with drugs or indulge in alcohol, feelings of frustration and despair are familiar. Fortunately, Meher Baba understood this and gave many encouraging messages as well as practical methods useful on our ongoing spiritual journey. Below are just a few of these selected for their association with the subject matter of this book.

ENCOURAGING MESSAGES:

> There is always hope for everyone; no one is utterly lost, and none need despair.[55]

- It is natural that at times you feel 100% miserable. Be sure that I know everything. When everything goes wrong the mind becomes helpless and has to rely solely on My help. When you leave all to Me, I dare not neglect you, and you get relief from your predicament. I am the Ocean of Love and Compassion.[56]

- Don't lose heart, but keep Me in your heart and remember I am always with you.[57]

- You fall, you stumble, falter, but if you don't fall, how will I be able to exercise my infinite compassion? Remember when you stumble, my hand is extended to lift you up.[58]

- ...do not let the fact of your depression depress you. Have you given thought as to where this depression was prior to its appearance? It has emerged unasked and as such it must vanish. Your forced efforts to overcome it will only imprint itself all the more on your mind and create further binding. So be completely indifferent to it and it will disappear.[59]

- To the struggling, falling and faltering humanity I say "have faith." Turn to God in complete surrenderance and receive the Divine Love. You are equally a part of the one indivisible divine life. There is not a single atom that does not vibrate with this divine life. There is no need for anyone to despair. The greatest of sinners as well as the greatest of saints has the same unfailing divine assurance.[60]

- The esoteric fact which I want you to remember is that the Beloved (God) is more keen and eager to realize the lover (man) than the latter's anxiety and longing for such a union.[61]

Even the worst sinners can become great saints if they have the courage and sincerity to invite a drastic and complete change of heart.[62]

- People ask God for forgiveness. But since God is everything and everyone, who is there for Him to forgive? Forgiveness of the created was already there in His act of creation.[63]

- Have no anxiety about any matter. Be brave; it will all pass away![64]

- I am ever conscious that I am you, while you are never conscious that I am in you. Daily I support you and share your consciousness.[65]

- Any time a person's thoughts turn truly to Me, I am truly with them.[66]

- The Master is himself beyond good or evil and is not perturbed by the failings of the disciple. He tolerates them with unfailing patience and infinite capacity to wait, knowing full well that once the disciple gets established on the path these failings will be swiftly washed away.[67]

- Do not worry about your weaknesses. Eventually they will go; even if they linger, love will one day consume them. Everything disappears in the Ocean of Love. Because I love you, you have a pool of love within you. When you feel wretched, when you fall in your weakness, have a dip in that pool of love. Refresh yourself in that pool of my love within you. It is always there.[68]

Practical Methods

- Every man must work out his own salvation, and must choose his own method, although his choice is mostly determined by the total effect of the mind impressions (sanskaras) acquired in previous lives. He should be guided by the creed of his conscience, and follow the method that best suits his spiritual tendency, his physical aptitude and his external circumstances. Truth is one, but the approach to it is essentially individual.[69]

- Honesty will guard you against false modesty and will give you the strength of true humility. Spare no pains to help others. Seek no other reward than the gift of Divine Love. Yearn for this gift sincerely and intensely, and I promise in the name of my Divine Honesty that I will give you much more than you yearn for.[70]

- Trust God completely and He will solve all your difficulties. Faithfully leave everything to Him and He will see to everything.[71]

- Keep your mind quiet, steady and firm. Do not submit to desires, but try to control them. One who cannot restrain his tongue cannot restrain his mind; one who cannot restrain his mind cannot restrain his action; one who cannot restrain his actions cannot restrain himself; and one who cannot restrain himself cannot attain his real Infinite Self.[72]

- Learn the art of taking your stand on the Truth within. When you live in this Truth, the result is the fusion of the mind and the heart and the end of all fears and sorrow. It is not a dry attainment of mere power or intellectual knowledge. A love which is illumined by the intuitive wisdom of the spirit will bless your life with ever-renewing fulfillment and never-ending sweetness.[73]

- The only Real Control is the discipline of

- the senses to abstain from indulgence in low desires, which alone ensures absolute purity of character.[74]

- Spiritual advancement is a succession of one surrender after another until the goal of the final surrenderance of the separate ego-life is completely achieved.[75]

- Think of things that you will not hesitate to think in My presence, speak words that you will not hesitate to speak in My presence and do things that you will not hesitate to do in My presence.[76]

- Sincere penance does not consist in perpetuating grief for the wrongs but in resolving to avoid in the future those deeds that call forth remorse. If it leads to lack of self-respect or self-confidence, it has not served its true purpose, which is merely to render impossible the repetition of certain types of action.[77]

- When you rise in the morning, think of Me for one second – just for one second – as if you were putting Me on as you put on your coat; again at 12 noon and at 5 pm, just as you might adjust your tie in a second, and finally the same at night, when getting into bed, which makes 4 seconds in all.[78]

- Try to see and feel me in everything and everyone. This is the real and direct method, but very, very few fortunate souls know it, much less work with its aid.[79]

- ...the most essential condition of spiritual advancement is the decreasing of egoism to its minimum. ... It is therefore most necessary for the aspirant to keep free from the idea "I do this, and I do that."...Thus he is caught up in a dilemma: if he stays inactive, he does nothing to break through the prison of his ego-life; and, if he takes to a life of action, he is faced with the possibility of his ego being transferred to these new acts.[80]

- To avoid inaction on the one hand and the pride of action on the other, it is necessary for the aspirant to construct in the following manner a provisional and working ego that will be entirely subservient to the Master. Before beginning anything, the aspirant thinks that it is not he who is doing it but the Master who is getting it done through him. After doing the task he does not tarry to claim the results of action or enjoy them but becomes free of them by offering them to the Master. By training his mind in this spirit, he succeeds in creating a new ego – which, though only provisional and working, is amply able to become a source of confidence, feeling, enthusiasm and "go" that true action must express. This new ego is spiritually harmless, since it derives its life and being from the Master, who represents Infinity. And when the time comes, it can be thrown away, like a garment.[81]

- The easiest and safest way to lose one's finite ego is by surrendering completely to the Perfect Master or the Avatar, who is consciously one with Truth. In them the past, present and future of the individual are drowned and during his implicit obedience to the master he is no longer bound by those actions, good and bad. Such complete surrenderance is in itself complete freedom.

A still more simple way to attain the Goal is to obey Me – obey Me implicitly. That is simpler than the simplest thing. Try, if you try, I will help you. Once you have determined to obey, you are no longer on your own. The slightest hypocrisy spoils your determination and makes the whole thing a farce.

The best course for My lover is to remember Me wholeheartedly as much as he can, and to remain happy. So try to love Me by remembering Me, and leave the rest to Me.[82]

- The most practical way for the common man to express this language of the heart, whilst attending to daily-life duties, is to speak lovingly, think lovingly, and act lovingly towards all mankind, irrespective of caste, creed and position, taking God to be present in each and every one.[83]

- Remember me, and I am there with you and My Love will guide you.[84]

Meher Baba gives us many reasons not to use drugs. In addition, he provides motivation and a spiritually grounded support system to help us move forward in life, toward the goal of spiritual self-realization, of who-you-really-are. He explains that it is not through external references (or substances) that we arrive at self-knowledge, but only by the total and complete embracing of the innermost Self. Furthermore, this spiritual path leading to the ultimate Reality is directly experienced by the spiritual aspirant in unfolding stages. Each stage of the journey brings a lasting and deepening experience of the Divine Presence within.[85] In other words, the journey toward Truth unfolds to the seeker immense joy and bliss in gradual stages, climaxing in the total realization of this Truth. This is the direct experience of the nature of the Soul, the knowledge that one is, in fact, Infinite in every way.

Although the world is rapidly moving toward a global culture that frequently seeks to escape from the lessons of life, Meher Baba indicated that a "New Humanity" would inherit the world, through spiritual guidance and direct experience. This New Humanity must have a thorough understanding of the dangers of drug abuse. Here Baba shares more about the spiritual awakening that will bring this new culture about:

> The New Humanity will come into existence through a release of love in measureless abundance, and this release of love can come through spiritual awakening brought about by the Masters.[86] Love cannot be born of mere determination; through the exercise of will one can at best be dutiful. Through struggle and effort, one may succeed in assuring that one's external action is in conformity with one's concept of what is right; but such action is spiritually barren because it lacks the inward beauty of spontaneous love. Love has to spring spontaneously from within; it is in no

way amenable to any form of inner or outer force. Love and coercion can never go together, but while love cannot be forced upon anyone, it can be awakened through love itself. Love is essentially self-communicative; those who do not have it catch it from those who have it. Those who receive love from others cannot be its recipients without giving a response which, in itself, is the nature of love. True love is unconquerable and irresistible. It goes on gathering power and spreading itself until eventually it transforms everyone it touches. Humanity will attain to a new mode of being and life through the free and unhampered interplay of pure love from heart to heart.[87]

6.

DIVINE INTOXICATION

ON THE SURFACE, a spiritual seeker and an addict (or alcoholic) may seem worlds apart, but upon closer examination there are some similarities. Even so, their differences produce vastly different outcomes. As Meher Baba says:

> The behavior of the drunkard and the lover are similar; each disregards the world's standards of conduct and each is indifferent to the opinion of the world. But there are worlds of difference between the course and the goal of the two: one leads to subterranean darkness and denial; the other gives wings to the soul for its flight to freedom.[88]

Meher Baba further compares the drunkard

and alcohol consumption with the lover of God who drinks the wine of pure Love:

> The drunkenness of the drunkard begins with a glass of wine which elates his spirit and loosens his affections and gives him a new view of life that promises a forgetfulness from his daily worries. He goes on from a glass to two glasses, to a bottle; from companionship to isolation, from forgetfulness to oblivion – oblivion, which in Reality is the original State of God, but which, with the drunkard, is an empty stupor – and he sleeps in a bed or in a gutter. And he awakens in a dawn of futility, an object of disgust and ridicule to the world.
>
> The lover's drunkenness begins with a drop of God's love, which makes him forget the world. The more he drinks, the closer he draws to his Beloved, and the more unworthy he feels of the Beloved's love; and he longs to sacrifice his very

life at his Beloved's feet. He, too, does not know whether he sleeps on a bed or in a gutter, and becomes an object of ridicule to the world; but he rests in bliss, and God the Beloved takes care of his body, and neither the elements nor disease can touch it."[89]

Meher Baba ultimately redirects addictive tendencies toward the life of the spirit.

> If you become addicted to God, then all your problems are solved. Go on drinking the Love of God until you become one with God.[90]

The great saints and ardent seekers of truth slowly develop an ever-increasing longing for God such as Baba described. This longing can and does become a healthy obsession for some, which enables them to give up the addiction not only to drugs, but to the very cosmic Illusion itself.

7.

VOICES OF EXPERIENCE

THE FOCUS OF THIS BOOK SO FAR has been to provide the reader with a comprehensive view of drug use in light of Meher Baba's wisdom and teaching. However, it is also extremely important to give those who have direct experience using drugs an opportunity to share, in hopes that their stories will offer yet another perspective on these spiritually important issues. Therefore, this section is devoted to individual, personal sharing related to drug use.

A man visits Meher Baba and says he is addicted to drugs.[91]

> Meher Baba: Are you happy?
>
> Man: No, very, very miserable.

Meher Baba: Never think that "Life is dreadful. I am tired of life."

Such thoughts make life miserable. Life is worth living. If you think it is, difficulties will appear insignificant. I will help you to try to develop love. Never think, "I am alone...."

ADDICT FROM A BABA FAMILY

I WAS BORN INTO A LOVING FAMILY of devout followers of Meher Baba in 1971. The first eight years of my life were spent surrounded by the Meher Baba community living near the Meher Spiritual Center in Myrtle Beach, South Carolina. I loved Baba all along. I knew what Baba said about drugs and their spiritual harmfulness. So how did I end up hopelessly addicted to drugs and alcohol? Well, I suppose my story is similar to that of many people from different religious and spiritual backgrounds.

Sometimes knowledge about drugs and even about spirituality is not enough.

When I was eight years old, our family moved to New York. It was a big adjustment for all of us, but eventually I settled in and enjoyed becoming a bona fide New Yorker. When junior high rolled around, I went from being very popular, vivacious, and happy, overnight it seemed, to being rejected by my peers, viciously teased, frightened, and feeling heavily betrayed by the world. I sought relief and help by taking my first trip to India in 1984. It was a great relief and comfort to me, as my relationship with Meher Baba deepened greatly within my heart when I felt his enveloping love and acceptance in his Tomb there. Nevertheless, when I returned to face school and the daily hell I lived in, I lost touch with those feelings and again sought escape.

At age fourteen I sought that escape and sense of freedom through boyfriends, drinking, and smoking pot. I felt a real acceptance among other kids who liked to party and seek oblivion. I was no longer walking on eggshells and feeling all those gut-ripping emotions. But as I drank and smoked pot, I started doing things I didn't really want to do. I started hanging out with people I didn't want to hang out with. I started sleeping with people I didn't want to sleep with, and before long I started doing drugs I didn't want to be doing. I began taking acid, doing cocaine and becoming less and less in control of my behavior and my feelings.

In 1988 I tried the India cure again. I was seventeen years old. I was already seeking help from two therapists. I was using every day, and I knew that I couldn't stop using on my own. I ran to Baba for help. The two weeks in India were wonderful. I was clean and I was reunited with my Beloved God, Meher Baba. I discovered a book there called *The Mastery of Consciousness* by Allan Y. Cohen. I devoured this book and took extensive notes. It seemed to be talking directly to me. Baba even blessed me with a spiritual experience inspired by a chapter in the book, to really get through to me the importance of remembrance and the use of the provisional ego. What I learned in that book was a method of getting closer to God called the provisional ego. What this means is that in order to avoid the traps of one's ego, we use a provisional ego, sort of a temporary ego, to buffer and protect ourselves. Practically, it meant I was to say to myself as I was walking down the hall, "Baba is walking down the hall"; as I was eating dinner, "Baba is eating dinner", etc., so as to detach myself from the harmful attachments of the ego and at the same time to be calling out to God throughout my day. Of course, this method will work with any name of God, as God is universal and beyond the universe.

I left India full of hope only to find myself back in the States and high within a week. For the next year and a half I continued downwards. At first I couldn't even look at Baba's face in the pictures on the walls for shame. But as my addiction progressed and my desperation increased, I began to seek Baba and to use the provisional ego as a last resort. I began saying to myself, "It is Baba using drugs," "Baba is buying drugs," "Baba is drunk," etc. It may seem bizarre but I believe it was this practice that eventually saved my life and led me to help and recovery. In the midst of that foggy year and a half, one of my therapists suggested I try Narcotics Anonymous. I went for a few months, decided I was too young, didn't do the right drugs, didn't believe alcohol was part of the problem, and left. Essentially, I still had some pride left.

In 1989 I moved down to Greensboro, North Carolina, to begin college. I had promised myself that I would stop drugs (alcohol not included, of course) a number of times and lasted up to a few weeks before getting high again. College was another reason to stop getting high and I told myself once I started college, I would turn over a new leaf. Of course, within no time I had found connections in Greensboro and was getting high regularly. The word that describes this period of my life better than any other is loneliness. I was so empty inside that I felt alone in every situation; by myself, with friends, in crowds. I was sick and tired of being sick and tired. I was lost and confused and felt totally out of control, hopeless, and scared. I had lost almost all sense of care for myself or my life.

Then came my miracle. God's Grace descended on me. I was looking around the neighborhood for an apartment, and I had spoken with two girls who were moving into an apartment to see if any more were available. They said there weren't, but we exchanged phone numbers just in case. I was a little fuzzy back then, so I don't recall if it was later that day or later that week, but my boyfriend and I were walking down the street and I literally heard a voice from within say, "There's a

Narcotics Anonymous meeting in that building across the street." I had given up on Narcotics Anonymous nine months before, had decided it didn't work, and had no intention of returning. Still, the voice was so powerful that I walked across the street and into the building. And there was a Narcotics Anonymous meeting in that building. I found out later that this meeting met once a week for one hour! And, as if that weren't enough, one of the girls I had met while looking for apartments was in that meeting. She became my sponsor, and I already had her phone number!

There is no doubt in my mind that God picked me up and put me in the right place and with the people that could help me. It still took a couple of months from that point until I totally cleaned up. That fateful and glorious day was over thirteen years ago and I haven't had to use drugs since. I was eighteen years old.

The story ends there and begins there, for my journey of self-recovery involved much, much more than simple (but not easy!) abstinence. It involved being around people who understood, loved, and accepted me and knew exactly how to help me recover because they had done it themselves. Ironically, after I got clean it took a long time for me to let God in again, as I had developed a lot of resentment against him during my addiction, calling out many times for help to a seemingly deaf ear. But once I did let him in again, and acknowledged the miracle he had given me, the love, mercy, and grace I felt from him were and continue to be overwhelming.

When I was younger I prided myself on being a rebel, someone who thought and lived outside the box of society, and when I gave up drugs I was afraid of becoming mediocre, a zombie of society. But what I came to discover is that real rebelliousness is something much greater. It involves having the courage to face life without a net and to experience life to the fullest, without buffering my feelings, and depending solely on

God for guidance and comfort. Reckless abandon was and still is my creed. Only now I try to recklessly abandon myself to God's will, and let me tell you, so far the ride is much smoother!

My story is just one of many, and the means of solving my problem is not the only one; it just happens to be the one that worked for me, and I believe Baba knew exactly what I needed. I hope that my story will help other kids from Baba families or from other families who may have had similar experiences to see that they are not alone and that there is hope. I believe those heartfelt connections I had with Baba throughout my life served as ground cables laid for the moment when I most needed and was most ready to receive his help. As Meher Baba says, "There is always hope for everyone; no one is utterly lost, and none need despair."[92] And further about God: "Keep Him ever constantly present within you. Let Him form the basis of all your thoughts, speech and actions. Remember

Him in every little thing you do – the responsibility will then rest with Him."[93]

– *L.K.S.*

A Teenager in New York City

I GREW UP IN MANHATTAN, in the West Village, and was in junior high school during the early 1980s. During the eighth grade I started using marijuana. At first I smoked very rarely, and soon after I smoked as often as I could. Some of my friends at school smoked as well, and some of them did not approve of my ways, but remained my friends.

I remember that my older sister, who was in high school, used drugs, including speed (amphetamines). I also knew that her boyfriend was dealing drugs. One night during this time we had a dance at our school. My sister had given me speed, just one blue pill, and my friend and I decided we would both use speed that night. I remember taking half the pill, because I was too scared of what it would do to me. The actual effect was that it filled me with enormous amounts of energy, which at the time I liked, so at some point in the evening I took the other half of the pill.

At the dance everyone was staring at me, because from what I heard later, I was dancing so fast that nobody could believe it, I had become a blur on the dance floor. I don't know exactly what happened, but somehow a teacher who was acting as a chaperone at the dance must have asked some of my classmates, and the information leaked out that I had taken some drug. The next day, I experienced the exact opposite effect, which was that I had absolutely no energy whatsoever. It was as if I had been completely drained of all energy, which I immediately understood as the down side of the high from the night before.

My school called my parents, and for the first time I was directly confronted about my drug use. My parents asked me point blank if I was using drugs, and I admitted yes, that I was smoking marijuana and had used speed. My father was furious; however, I happened to know that he also smoked marijuana, and I confronted him about this, since it seemed hypocritical to me. His anger was such that he directly threatened me, saying that if I continued to use drugs he would "come down on me like God!" This made an impression on me, but not a very deep one.

I decided that I did not like speed (because the down was not worth the up) and never used it again. But I continued to use marijuana for years after this, until my father's death in 1985. His death was profoundly troubling to me, and I spent about six months drinking a lot of alcohol and smoking a lot of pot, and hash if I could get any. Then in late 1985 I came to know of Meher Baba in Manhattan. When I learned that Baba had said not to use drugs, and that he required his disciples and followers to be drug free, I immediately felt inspired to go beyond my drug dependency. Within six months, with Baba's help, I had given up drugs entirely.

Through my relationship with Meher Baba I have not used any drugs at all since 1986 (unless you consider coffee a drug). While beer and wine are not illegal, I still feel it is important for me not to drink more than one or two glasses on any given occasion. However, after returning from India in July 2001, I felt I should try to give up my attachment to drinking alcohol. The feeling is that, even in small amounts, my attachment to alcohol gets in the way of my deepening relationship with Baba. Since my father was an alcoholic, this issue has been particularly charged. This is my new challenge, and I have asked Meher Baba to please help me overcome alcohol, once and for all.

– *L.W.*

From Foggy to Light

I GREW UP IN RURAL SOUTH GEORGIA under a heavy blanket of Christianity. Not that my parents were Bible thumpers, the blanket existed long before their time. We went to church, I believe, because it is what my dad thought we were supposed to do and what I think my mom felt to be right in her heart. I went to a Christian school from kindergarten through ninth grade. I have always been very fond of animals, and growing up on a farm allowed me to survive what at the time I thought was an unbearable childhood. Animals were my best friends. I specifically remember asking my Bible teacher one day what happened to all the animals when they died, and she told me since they did not have souls they would go to hell. I was crushed. I was torn. I really loved God and had been praying ever since I could remember for God to allow me to be the caretaker of the animal kingdom in heaven. I had such a beautiful image for such a long time and I would pray to God every night to say hello to my animal friends who had died. It was really hard for me to accept that God could allow something so awful as letting animals burn in hell.

Being so young, I don't remember all the details, but I do know a couple of years later I seriously began to doubt God. I think I was about thirteen, and my horse had been chronically and incurably ill for some time. I could not agree to putting him down. I remember asking God to please let me have his sickness so that he could stop suffering. I would devise tests to try and prove whether or not God was listening to me. My faith was waning and my tests were no longer about whether God was listening, but whether God was even real. Finally, one day when my mom picked me up from school, she told me my horse had died. I had never been so heartbroken. I was so lost and confused.

By the time I graduated from high school, I did

not believe in God at all. For a few years I maintained this attitude, until I had a spiritual experience on LSD. I don't even remember what it was during that trip except that I felt like there was something out there and that it was a huge and beautiful something. I had been using drugs for several years, always searching for something, always trying to get free. At this particular time, I had stopped going to college and was in Santa Cruz, California. I had gotten pretty self-righteous in my drug use, believing that altered states of consciousness were the only way to live.

I traveled around the United States following the Grateful Dead and Jerry Garcia Band for several years. I hitchhiked all over the country constantly putting myself in dangerous situations. I prided myself on having found the key – beautiful music and LSD. I tried to convince myself of this for a long time. I believed I was very spiritual. My drug use grew and so did my loneliness. Even though I was usually surrounded by swarms of hippie families, I felt so alone. The feelings I was trying not to feel through my drug use were killing me, but I never admitted anything to anyone.

In the early 1990s I once again tried a geographical cure. My drug use had elevated and I could no longer convince even myself that things were magical, spiritual, and beautiful. Some drugs no matter how you look at them are ugly. Those were the drugs I found myself doing in San Francisco. My new blame was Babylon. I told myself that if I could just get out of the city, all would be well. With money from selling drugs, I bought a one-way ticket to Hawaii from a girl in the parking lot of the New Year's Eve Grateful Dead show in Oakland, California.

I must admit, a tropical island paradise is about the best geographical cure one could make. Maybe that is one of the reasons that when it turned ugly once again, I truly felt hopeless. I had found something so beautiful and had cleaned myself up for a couple of months, only doing the "organic" drugs. I had a spiritual awakening in Hawaii and felt really connected to something greater than me. I felt a deep reverence for the Earth, and the ocean saved me from myself, but only for a time. No matter where I went, there I was. The cycle was always the same. I was kidding no one; I was totally out of control. I believe in those years when I was running all over the country, believing I had found freedom in my total self-centeredness, that God was always looking out for me. I had many spiritual experiences and short moments of clarity. When I was presented with a possible opportunity to travel East on a drug trafficking mission, somehow, I opted not to go and instead returned to my home in rural South Georgia.

Once again, I tried to convince myself that I could clean up out in the country (where I grew up and no drugs existed) and I could get it together. I cleaned up for a short while and then called up friends in California to send me what I wanted. I was insane. I left for Greensboro, North Carolina, a few months later, believing that if I went back to college, all would be well. Again, a couple of months of doing just the "organics" and I thought I had everything under control. The denial was so huge. In no time at all, I was involved with a crowd that was doing a drug that I had been romanticizing about for years. I was really sick and went down really fast, much further than I had been down before.

In another divine intervention, I called my mom and, hysterically crying, told her I could not stop doing drugs. My parents had over the years tried several times to get me help, but I always refused. The mother of one of my friends in Greensboro happened to be a substance abuse counselor. I guess my mother's instinct told her she had really better do what she could this time, and the next day she arrived in town. My junkie "friends" vacated my house, and my mom, my friend, and her mother who was the substance abuse counselor ended up at dinner one night. To my dismay they were discussing a treatment center that I would be going to. Once again, I refused. I tried to convince them that I did not have a drug problem. After much pleading and bargaining, I agreed to attend one Narcotics Anonymous meeting if I found that I could not stay off of drugs. A couple of days later after I had been again using against my will, I called the number my friend's mom had given me. I went to a Narcotics Anonymous meeting for myself for the first time, and when it came time to introduce myself, the words "My name is Larissa and I am an addict" flew out of my mouth and I broke down.

At that meeting there were several women who reached out to me, gave me their phone numbers, and told me I didn't have to use again. I didn't believe that I was capable of a life without drugs, wasn't sure that was what I wanted, and I sure didn't believe these women had a drug problem like I did. I just wanted some relief and I had gotten it at that meeting. For the first time in a long time, I had a crumb of hope. True hope. I kept coming back to the meetings and eventually asked one of these women to be my sponsor.

Through the years and all my using I had gotten so confused about God and spirituality. In the end of my active addiction, I had been thanking God for my drugs. My whole life was so foggy and painful. Once I stopped the drugs and began to clear up, I was really attracted to the life my sponsor had. She seemed to be truly free and she wasn't a nerd either, like I had expected non-druggies to be. I began to get to know her and she told me about Meher Baba. I was intrigued, but hesitant. I was inquisitive, yet reluctant. She told me stories of her personal experiences and stories she had heard from other Baba-lovers or books about Baba. I remember her showing me a picture of Meher Baba she had taped in her Narcotics

Anonymous Basic Text, and she pointed to it and said, "He is my Higher Power."

Before I knew it, Meher Baba had snuck into my heart. I loved to hear stories about him and relished reading the poetry of Hafiz with my friend. I would have dreams about Baba. My friend would give me books about Baba, which I would devour (except for the Discourses) and pictures of him with little sayings to keep. In 1997, my friend decided to move back to New York and I decided to go check out a commune in Summertown, Tennessee. With less than two years clean I lived at the commune and with Baba's grace stayed clean. It was another confusing time in my life. Thankfully, I had Baba to lean on. I had gotten used to asking for help from Baba. I would look at his picture and carry on a heart-to-heart conversation with him. I knew in my heart that Baba loved me no matter what and would help me anytime.

Eventually, a door opened and I moved to

Nashville, where there were tons of Narcotics Anonymous meetings and the fellowship was very strong. Doors continued to open for me and in February of 2000 I went to India. If I wasn't sure of my love and devotion for Meher Baba before, I was convinced once I was in Meherabad. Baba melted my heart there. I totally surrendered to him and was willing to do anything he wanted of me. I always had a hunger for revelations and huge, spontaneous changes in my life. I was ready to leave my boyfriend, career, pets, not to mention my family back in the States, but Baba said no, "Do not shirk your worldly duties". I surrendered again, to the fact that Baba is in everything and everywhere. I do not have to continue searching, turning everything upside down. As I learned from Baba, the treasure is within. I am clear, the fog has lifted, and Meher Baba is my light. He was always there in one form or another, but I was too busy medicating and running. I have never felt so free. I am so grateful to Baba and so grateful to my friend who introduced me to Baba and for the way Baba worked through her to sneak into my heart.

– *L.L.*

Jim's Story

THIS IS DEDICATED TO ALL PEOPLE searching for hope and meaning in their lives. My name is Jim Bender. I am a recovering addict/alcoholic who has been in recovery for over nineteen years. I am forty-three years old and am married to a beautiful woman named Kimberly. We have one child, a son named Logan, born on December 23, 2002. I want to share with you a little of my life before being introduced to Baba.

I was raised in a large Catholic family, four sisters and one brother. My mother raised us and my father worked for the U.S. government as a contractor responsible for building anti-ballistic missile systems. We spent several years outside the continental U.S. while I was a teenager. I was exposed to many different cultures and races of people at an early age. In my eyes, people were people. This is where my association with drugs and alcohol began. I took acid, uppers, downers, drank alcohol and smoked lots of pot while overseas. I never thought it was abnormal or unusual for a ten-year-old to be getting high and drunk. All my friends did it. My parents were too busy involving themselves in their own social activities to notice my involvement in the drug subculture. Or so I thought! I got caught sneaking beer from my dad's refrigerator one night. He was very surprised and shocked. How could a good Catholic boy do such a thing? I received a good talking to that night. He thought I would never touch another beer again. Boy, was he wrong! I just got better at hiding and covering up my use and abuse from people who loved me the most. This is a crucial mistake I kept making during my downward spiral toward death from addiction and alcoholism: covering up my use and making excuses to myself to keep on using despite all the negative consequences. My drinking and using drugs got progressively worse until in desperation I cried out for help. That was on March 7, 1984, and I have not found it necessary to drink or use drugs since that day. I hope you will allow yourself the same opportunity to stop using drugs and find a wonderful way to live through Baba and his unconditional Love.

I have known about Baba for over twelve years. I was introduced to him by a friend who showed me a picture of him while we were attending an Alcoholics Anonymous meeting. The first time I saw him, I asked my friend, "Who is this man and why do you carry a picture of him?" She replied, "This is GOD and you can have his picture if you want it." I was shocked at her response. I did not believe her at first. How could she possess a picture of GOD! I thought for a moment he looked like a pizza deliveryman, what with that bushy moustache and big nose. I started to laugh. This shows the arrogance I possessed at this time. I had a concept of GOD in my mind, and it did not gel with the image I saw in front of me.

I am so grateful to Baba and my friend that I was allowed to come to understand Baba as I understand him, slowly and gently. This is the example of how the greatest actor in the universe, Baba, won my heart. He came to me the only way he could, under the disguise of a pizza deliveryman. Oh, the humor of it all.

Several years later I had the opportunity to visit the Meher Spiritual Center in Myrtle Beach. This is where I had a very special dream about Baba. In my dream, I approached several men who were sitting on the ground under some huge shade trees. They were all dressed in white, barefoot, smiling at me. I recall knowing who these men were and especially who one of them was. He was Baba. He motioned for me to approach him, and I blurted out before I knew what else to say: "Baba, what do I have to do to follow you?" Baba didn't speak with his mouth; he thought his answer into my heart. His answer to my question was this: "GET RID OF YOUR TENNIS SHOES AND COME FOLLOW ME". I remember waking up and suddenly the memory of my dream became overwhelming and frightful. I immediately went out on the deck of my hotel room and looked out over the Atlantic Ocean. The moon was high in the sky, with thousands of stars overhead. I knew this was a real encounter. I had been asking for a sign from Baba for several months. My friend had said many times to me, be careful what you ask for, you might just get it. Well, I did that night. Many times I have asked people what this dream could have possibly meant. I still don't know for sure. Everyone has a different answer. I think in some mysterious way Baba is asking me to rid myself of all the material, ego-driven ways I followed in this world. What do you think?

One thing is for sure, I would not be in a position I am in now to share with you my experiences about Baba if I hadn't quit using all mood – and mind-altering drugs. The use of any drug other than for medical purposes prescribed by a doctor causes any human to be cut off from the only source of Love in the universe, Baba. He is the only source of LOVE that I consider to be valid in this world of illusion. All other forms are False Emotions Appearing Real. I hope my story will lead you to ask the same question we all ask at some point in our lives. What is the meaning of life and where are we all headed? The answer for me is BABA, BABA.

– *J.B.*

Kendra's Confession

When I first encountered Meher Baba, I was stoned out of my mind on hashish.

I was not consciously a spiritual seeker at the

time, so I figure I must have fortunately stumbled into the path of Baba's Seclusion Work, which he was doing during that period (1968) in India.

At the time, I was twenty-two years old and living with my first husband in an apartment in Jerusalem. We were sitting, stoned, in our respective armchairs in the living room, he drawing in a sketchpad and I musing in a state of intoxicated reverie. Suddenly, out of nowhere, I had a very powerful vision of Divine Love. I felt love continuously pouring down on everyone and everything. I understood that the only important thing in life was to receive it and reflect it back to God and to others.

It was as if I were way up high, alongside "God," who was showing me all the people "down there," most of them unaware or ignorant of Him, though He loved them so much. He gave me to understand that there is nothing we have to do to earn His love—and there is nothing we can do to make Him withdraw that love. It is unconditional.

Following this experience, the feeling of being intensely high was gone. I later concluded that the vision was not caused by the intoxication but took place in spite of it. It was a life-changing experience that has stayed with me and grown, which can hardly be said of any other experience I ever had while using drugs.

A couple of weeks after it happened, I got a letter from a friend in the States telling me about Meher Baba. When I returned home to New York City a month later, I went to a meeting, bought and read the Discourses, and was instantly a Baba-lover. I recognized in Meher Baba the One who had contacted me in my vision.

I wish I could say that I immediately gave up drugs for all time in response to Baba's prohibition, but some habits are not easy to break. It took a few more years and the avoidance of marijuana-smoking friends before I was fully able to obey Baba's directives on drug use. Lyn Ott once told me something that I find comforting in this regard. He said, "Baba teaches you obedience by giving you the experience of disobedience."

– *K.C.B.*

If you have a personal story regarding your direct experience with drugs that you would like to see shared here in a future edition please send it to:

>Sheriar Foundation
>807 34th Ave South.
>N. Myrtle Beach, SC 29582 USA

8.

MEHER BABA: THE HIGHEST OF THE HIGH

MERWAN S. IRANI, named Meher Baba ("The Compassionate One") by his early disciples, was born in 1894 in Poona (now Pune), India. Between 1913 and 1921, the five Perfect Masters (Sadgurus) of the time unveiled to him his identity and universal mission as the Avatar of the Age (the God-Man, Christ, Rasool, Buddha). After working intensively from 1921 onwards with a group of early close disciples, Meher Baba began to observe silence in 1925, and throughout the more than four decades of his continuous spiritual activity and work, he did not utter a word. From his work in India and the East with the mad, the infirm, the poor and with spiritually advanced souls, to his contact with thousands in the West through thirteen trips between the 1930s and the 1950s, Baba has awakened innumerable persons to the quest for the realization of God as one's own Infinite Reality – all in Silence.

Throughout the years, Meher Baba indicated that the breaking of his silence would come in a way and at a time that one could not imagine, and that his "speaking the Word" after great chaos and confusion in the world would be his only miracle in this incarnation as God in human form. "When I break My Silence, the impact will jolt the world out of its spiritual lethargy... What will happen when I break My Silence is what has never happened before... The breaking of My Silence will reveal to man the universal Oneness of God, which will bring about the universal brotherhood of man."

The Avatar comes on earth as man to refresh the example of the highest ideals of human life, and to reawaken mankind to the possibility of establishing internal connections with God, the Divine Beloved in every heart. In his unlimited universality, he alone can give to Creation the internal push required to true its course. In his lifetime on earth he sows the seeds of selfless love where they must inevitably blossom and flourish, and he leaves behind his message and his example to help mankind fulfill the promise of its evolution and inner spiritual development. In this age, he provided unprecedented and crucial insight into the effects of psychoactive drugs at a time when humanity was at a critical crossroads in regard to experimenting with them.

In the 1960s, owing to the interest among many of his younger lovers in the psychedelic drugs that were popular at the time, Meher Baba spoke out about the potential harmfulness of using any drugs that were not taken specifically for legitimate medical conditions as prescribed by a doctor. His statements concerning the illusory nature of the experiences induced by drugs ranging from marijuana to LSD became the bedrock upon which many seekers established their own perspectives about real spirituality and began to pursue higher consciousness without the distractions and dangers of such drugs.

Declaring that his work had been completed 100 percent to his satisfaction and that the results would soon begin to manifest, Meher Baba dropped his body on January 31, 1969. According to his longstanding instructions, his human form was buried in the Tomb-Shrine (known as the Samadhi) that he had had built in the 1940s, atop Meherabad Hill outside Ahmednagar, India (about two hundred miles northeast of Bombay, or Mumbai). Since 1969 pilgrims from around the world have visited Meher Baba's Samadhi for the opportunity to imbibe the atmosphere of his love and presence there.

The above material about Meher Baba has

been excerpted from the Meher Baba Information website www.meherbabainformation.org, copyright © 2002 by Meher Baba Information. Used by permission.

GOD IN A PILL? REVISITED

THE FOLLOWING QUOTATIONS are reproduced from the pamphlet *God in a Pill?*, for the sake of historical continuity and future reference. We did not reproduce every quote from Meher Baba that is printed in *God in a Pill?*, as some of the quotes there are not directly related to drug use. In reference to the history of the pamphlet, Don Stevens mentions, "It might be of interest that when Baba indicated that he would like his various communications on drugs to be collected and issued as a small pamphlet, it was to Murshida Duce that he sent this suggestion. She in turn called me, as I was living in the San Francisco area at the time, and she asked me if I would take on the job."[94]

The title *God in a Pill?* came from Meher Baba's saying "If God can be found in a pill, then God is not worthy of being God."[95]

> In an age when individual liberty is prized above all achievements, the fast-increasing number of drug addicts forms an appalling chain of self-sought bondage! Even as these drugs hold out an invitation to a fleeting sense of ecstasy, freedom or escape, they enslave the individual in greater binding. LSD, a highly potent "mind changing" drug differing from the opiate derivatives and being used in the research of mental science, is said to "expand consciousness and alter one's personality for the better." In America it has become tragically popular among the young, used indiscriminately by any and many. They must be persuaded to desist from taking drugs, for they are harmful – physically, mentally and spiritually.

- All so-called spiritual experiences generated by taking 'mind-changing' drugs such as LSD, mescaline and psilocybin are superficial and add enormously to one's addiction to the deceptions of illusion, which is but the shadow of Reality.

- No drug, whatever its great promise, can help one to attain the spiritual goal. There is no short-cut to the goal except through the grace of the Perfect Master, and drugs, LSD more than others, give only a semblance of "spiritual experience," a glimpse of a false Reality.

- The experience of a semblance of freedom that these drugs may temporarily give to one is in actuality a millstone round the aspirant's neck in his efforts towards emancipation from the rounds of birth and death.

- The experience is as far removed from

Reality as is a mirage from water. No matter how much one pursues the mirage one will never reach water, and the search for truth through drugs must end in disillusionment. One who knows the Way, who is the Way, cannot approve the continued pursuance of a method that not only must prove fruitless but leads away from the Path that leads to Reality.

- Experiences gained through LSD are, in some cases, experiences of the shadows of the subtle (emotion, energy) plane in the gross (physical) world. These experiences have nothing at all to do with spiritual advancement.

- The user of LSD can never reach subtle consciousness in this incarnation despite its repeated use. To experience real spiritual consciousness, surrenderance to a Perfect Master is necessary.

- It is human, and therefore necessarily wrong-sighted, to view the result of the drug by its immediate relative effects – to calculate its end result is beyond human knowledge, and only the true Guide can point the way.

- The experiences derived through the drugs are experiences by one in the gross world of the shadows of the subtle planes and are not continuous. The experiences of the subtle sphere by one on the subtle planes are continuous, but even these experiences are of illusion, for Reality is beyond them. And so, though LSD may lead one to feel a better man personally, the feeling of having had a glimpse of Reality may not only lull one into a false security but also will in the end derange one's mind. Although LSD is not an addiction-forming drug, one can become attached to the experiences arising from its use and one gets tempted to use it in increasing doses, again and again, in the hope of deeper and deeper experiences. But eventually this causes madness or death.

- There is also a state of perverted consciousness. It is a state in which consciousness indulges in induced experiences such as those gotten from the use of drugs; even the most fantastic experiences thus induced are only the shadows of the subtle plane experienced in the gross world.

- Only the One who knows and experiences Reality, who is Reality, has the ability and authority to point out the false from the Real. The only Real experience is to continuously see God within oneself as the infinite effulgent ocean of Truth and then to become one with this infinite ocean and continuously experience infinite knowledge, power and bliss.

∽ To a few sincere seekers, LSD may have served as a means to arouse that spiritual longing which has brought them into my contact, but once that purpose is served further ingestion would not only be harmful but have no point or purpose. The longing for Reality cannot be sustained by further use of drugs but only by the love for the Perfect Master which is a reflection of his love for the seeker.

∽ An individual may feel LSD has made a "better" man of him socially and personally. But one will be a better man through Love than one can ever be through drugs or any other artificial aid. And the best man is he who has surrendered himself to the Perfect Master irrespective of his personal or social standing.

As for possible use of the drug by an enlightened society for spiritual purposes – an enlightened society would never dream of using it!

- All the experiences even of spiritual aspirants on the Path to God-realization (gotten in the natural course of involution of consciousness) are of the domain of Illusion and are ephemeral and absolutely unimportant; how much more illusory and distracting are the experiences through substances compounded in a laboratory which have the semblance of those of the aspirant on the Spiritual Path! The one and only true experience is the experience of the Truth, the Reality; for once the realization of God is attained it remains a continual and never-ending experience.

- The all-pervading effulgence of God the Reality can only be experienced by an aspirant who keeps himself scrupulously above all illusory experimentations and humbly takes refuge in love of God.

- It is absolutely essential for a spiritual aspirant who genuinely longs for union with God – the Reality – to shun experiments with the effects of certain drugs. These things do not uplift the aspirant nor draw him out of the rut of Illusion. Experiences born of these practices wear off as soon as the aspirant withdraws from or is thrown out of the orbit of the effect produced by the technique employed.

- But there is no drug that can promote the aspirant's progress – nor ever alleviate the sufferings of separation from his beloved God. LOVE is the only propeller and the only remedy. The aspirant should love God with all his heart till he forgets himself and recognizes his beloved God in himself and others.

- Even the experiences of the planes of consciousness are only another kind of an illusion! Experiences of the planes are "Real Illusion," whereas those derived from the use of drugs are a "dream into a dream"; whereas the traversing of the spiritual Path by the seekers who gain experiences of planes of consciousness is a "dream."

- Medically there are legitimate uses of LSD. It can be used beneficially for chronic alcoholism, for severe and serious cases of depression and for relief in mental illnesses. Use of LSD other than for specific medical purposes is harmful physically, mentally and spiritually.

- Any drug when used medically for diseases, under the direct supervision of a medical practitioner, is not impermissible and cannot be classed with individual usage of a drug for what one can get out of it – or hope to get out of it – whether thrills, forgetfulness, or a delusion of spiritual experience.

- *LSD and other psychedelic drugs should never be used except when prescribed by a professional medical practitioner in the case of serious mental disorder under his direct supervision.*

- In short, LSD can be used beneficially for specific medical purposes, but for spiritual progress it is not only useless but positively *harmful*.

- If the student world continues to indulge in the use of LSD, the best of its intellectual potential will be lost to the nation.

- Use of LSD produces hallucinations, and prolonged use of this drug will lead to mental derangement, which even the medical use of LSD would fail to cure.

∽ Taking LSD is harmful physically, mentally and spiritually. But if you take me into your heart and love me as your real Self, you will find me in you as the infinite Ocean of Love. And this experience will remain continuously throughout eternity.

WHERE TO GET MORE INFORMATION

SUGGESTED READING

RECOVERY:
- *The Addictive Personality: Understanding the Addictive Process and Compulsive Behavior,* by Craig Nakken
- *Newsweek* February 2001, cover story is Abuse In America: The War on Addiction

BOOKS BY MEHER BABA:
- *God Speaks*, Meher Baba, Searchlight Books (www.slbooks.com)
- *Discourses*, Meher Baba, Sheriar Foundation (www.sheriarbooks.org)

- *Life at Its Best*, Meher Baba, Sufism Reoriented (www.slbooks.com)
- *Listen, Humanity*, Meher Baba, Crossroad Press (www.sheriarbooks.org)
- *The Everything and The Nothing*, Meher Baba, Sheriar Foundation (www.sheriarbooks.org)
- *Beams from Meher Baba on the Spiritual Panorama*, Meher Baba (www.slbooks.com)
- *Lord Meher: The Biography of the Avatar of the Age*, Meher Baba (20 vols.), Bhau Kalchuri, MANifestation, Inc.

Places of Interest

RECOVERY:

- Alcoholics Anonymous: AA Meeting Information throughout the U.S. provided online at http://soberspace.com/. *Also see*

the online Intergroup of Alcoholics Anonymous at http://aa-intergroup.org/.
- AnonymousOne: A recovery resource like no other at www.sobertoo.com.
- Narcotics Anonymous: www.na.org.
- An online directory for Mental Health and Sober Living at http://soberrecovery.com.
- Norchem Drug Testing Laboratory. A great reference site for drug testing and substance abuse information at http://www.norchemlab.com

SPIRITUALITY:

Some of the many Avatar Meher Baba web sites:
- Avatar Meher Baba Trust in India: www.ambppct.org
- Meher Spiritual Center in Myrtle Beach: www.mehercenter.org
- The first major Meher Baba site: www.avatarmeherbaba.org

- A page full of Meher Baba sites:
  www.avatarmeherbaba.com/babasites.html
- Another Meher Baba web site:
  www.meherbaba.com
- A recent addition to Meher Baba online:
  www.jaibaba.com

GENERAL SPIRITUALITY:

United Communities of Spirit at
http://origin.org/ucs.cfm

OTHER MEHER BABA ORGANIZATIONS:

MEHER BABA INFORMATION
www.meherbabainformation.org
PO Box 1101
Berkeley, CA 94701
Email: meherbabai@aol.com

MEHER SPIRITUAL CENTER
www.mehercenter.org
10200 Hwy 17. N.
Myrtle Beach, SC 29572
(843) 272-5777
Email: gateway@mehercenter.org

GLOW INTERNATIONAL
www.belovedarchives.org
7 Whitney Place
Princeton Junction, NJ 08550–2302
(609) 716–1296
Email: Zenocom@aol.com

LOVESTREET BOOKSTORE
www.lovestreetbookstore.com
Avatar Meher Baba Center of Southern CA
1214 S. Van Ness Ave.
Los Angeles, CA 90019-3520
(310) 837-6419
Email: Baba Book@pacbell.net

SEARCHLIGHT BOOKS
www.slbooks.com
PO Box 5552
Walnut Creek, CA 94596
(925) 934–9365
Email: sales@slbooks.com

SHERIAR BOOKS
www.sheriarbooks.org
807 34th Ave. S.
North Myrtle Beach, SC 29582
(843) 272–1339
Email: laura@sheriarbooks.org

GLOSSARY

acid: See LSD

amphetamines:
Amphetamines belong to a group of drugs (psychostimulants) which stimulate the central nervous system and speed up the messages going to and from the brain to the body. Amphetamines are therefore commonly known as *"speed,"* and come in different forms which can be taken in different ways. Most often amphetamines come as a white, yellow or brown powder in tablets, capsules, crystals, or red liquid. Amphetamines can be smoked, swallowed, inhaled through the nose ("snorted"), or dissolved in water and injected.

HARMFUL EFFECTS: See *methamphetamine* harmful effects.

bidis (or *beedis*): (Hindi) Big tobacco leaves hand rolled into a cigarette shape, tied with a thread, and smoked. Basically, an unfiltered cigarette. Active ingredient is nicotine.

HARMFUL EFFECTS: Because nicotine is so addictive, it is extremely hard to give up smoking. Nicotine has two effects on the central nervous system, first stimulation and then sedation. The sense of fatigue which the sedation brings causes continued smoking. Smokers experience a high rate of lung cancer, emphysema, and other potentially deadly diseases.

bhang, also bhang–ganja: (Hindi) Bhang is an intoxicating drink made from poppy seeds (an opiate). Bhang-ganga is a drink made from *ganja. See also* marijuana.

charas: (Hindi) *Charas* literally means an intoxicating drug prepared from the flowers of hemp. A *charasi* is one who smokes it. According to Robert Dreyfuss, charas is what is known as hashish, not to be confused with ganja *(marijuana)*.

chillum: (Hindi) A pipe for smoking.

Effulgence: Light, radiance, glow, brilliance; used to connote the Light of God.

Enlightenment: (Buddhism) A final blessed state marked by the absence of desire or suffering. *See also* God-Realization.

ecstasy: A very popular club drug used by many teenagers. This drug has characteristics of both methamphetamine and hallucinogens. The active ingredient is MDMA (methylenedioxymethamphetamine).

HARMFUL EFFECTS: Some degree of long-term damage to areas of the brain specifically related to thinking and memory. One or more of the following may result from usage: confusion, depression, trouble sleeping, deep anxiety, paranoia, psychotic episodes, muscle tension, bruxism (clenching of teeth), nausea, blurred vision, faintness, chills, increased heart rate, and increased blood pressure.

ganja: (Hindi) *See* marijuana.

ghazal: A Persian or Urdu poem or song composed in a particular form. The Spiritual Master and poet Hafiz of Shiraz perfected the ghazal form.

God–Man: The Prophet, Avatar, Buddha, Christ of the age. This man is literally "God in human form," and becomes recognized as such by humanity at large as the greatest spiritual figure of his time. Meher Baba indicated that Zoroaster, Rama, Krishna, Buddha, Jesus, and Muhammad were all incarnations of the one God-Man, and that he was also this same Ancient One incarnate.

God-Realization: The state of union with God. Meher Baba explained that this state of consciousness is continuous (without a break), and that it is the experience of Infinite Knowledge, Infinite Power, and Infinite Bliss. A Perfect Master experiences God-realization every moment.

hallucination: The perception of objects with no reality, usually arising from a disorder of the nervous system or in response to drugs. A related effect is a "delusion," an unfounded or mistaken impression, thought, or notion,

hallucinogen: Any substance that induces hallucinations as a frequent side effect. Hallucinogenic drugs include LSD, mescaline, psilocybin, and strong dosages of THC (contained in marijuana and hasish).

hashish (or *hash*): A resinous byproduct of the marijuana plant which produces intoxication when smoked or eaten. The active ingredient is tetrahydrocannabinol (THC). *See also* charas; marijuana.

hemp: Hemp used to create rope, furniture, clothing, paper, and other products is not a narcotic. The scientific name for marijuana is *cannabis hemp*, as it is from the hemp family. What makes marijuana a narcotic is the presence of THC (tetrahydrocannabinol). But not all hemp plants contain THC levels high enough to qualify them as a narcotic. In short, all marijuana is hemp, but not all hemp is marijuana.

heroin: An opiate that is manufactured primarily from morphine–like molecules in opium, heroin is a powerful drug close to morphine in structure and ultimately metabolized into morphine by the body. In the body, heroin is metabolized into morphine within a few hours, and there are specific drug tests available to confirm the use of heroin.

HARMFUL EFFECTS: Heroin use by injection may result in collapsed veins, heart infection, liver disease, and other infectious diseases including HIV/AIDS. Heroin is highly addictive, and an overdose may result in death. During pregnancy its use may cause spontaneous abortion. See also opiates.

LSD: A hallucinogen, LSD (lysergic acid diethylamide) was discovered in 1938 by Dr. Albert Hofmann. It is a potent and very dangerous mood – and perception-altering chemical. It is made from lysergic acid, which is naturally found in ergot, a fungus that grows on grains. LSD, commonly referred to as "acid," is sold on the street in tablets, capsules, and occasionally liquid form. It has no odor or color, but may have a slightly bitter taste and is usually swallowed. Those intoxicated by LSD are said to be "tripping" or "on a trip."

HARMFUL EFFECTS: In some instances, fatal accidents have occurred during LSD intoxication. LSD users are at much greater risk of developing long–lasting psychoses, such as schizophrenia, severe depression, or other severe mental illness. LSD users may experience debilitating flashbacks (recurrences of the effects of LSD even long after its original use).

Mandali: (Hindi) Literally, of the circle, meaning a circle of disciples. Meher Baba indicated that a Perfect Master (Man-God) has a circle of 12 men and 2 women disciples for a total of 14. He further elucidated that the Avatar (God-Man) has ten circles of 12 disciples (both men and women), plus 2 women disciples in the innermost circle for a total of 122. (Rick Chapman indicates that *mandali* actually derives from the Marathi word for "close ones, family members, members of the household" according to Eruch's comments through various anecdotes about Meher Baba over the years. The primary thrust of the word as Meher Baba used it, according to Eruch, was "intimate ones," or those close to him in the way that family is close.)

marijuana: Leaves of the hemp plant, *cannabis sativa*, usually smoked in a pipe or rolled into cigarette form. Classified as a "hallucinogen," marijuana is one of the most popular drugs in America. The active ingredient in marijuana is tetrahydrocannabinol (THC).

HARMFUL EFFECTS: Lungs: unrelated to the THC levels, tar and carbon monoxide are inhaled and absorbed at three to five times greater levels than among tobacco smokers. Brain: deterioration of that part of the brain that is crucial for learning, memory, and integrating external experiences with feelings or emotions. Pregnancy: Research shows that babies of women who used marijuana during pregnancy have been born with some degree of neurological underdevelopment. General: impaired attention, memory, and learning ability.

methamphetamine:
Methamphetamine is an addictive stimulant drug that strongly activates certain systems in the brain. It is closely related chemically to amphetamine but affects the central nervous system more strongly. It is referred to as "speed, meth," and "chalk." Methamphetamine hydrochloride, looks like clear chunky crystals, and is referred to as "ice," "crystal," and "glass." It can be smoked.

HARMFUL EFFECTS: Methamphetamine abuse appears to damage brain cells over time, which can result in symptoms like those of Parkinson's disease (a severe disorder of the nerves). It can cause irreversible damage to blood vessels, resulting in cardiovascular collapse producing strokes or even death. Side effects may include irritability, insomnia, confusion, tremors, convulsions, anxiety, paranoia, aggressiveness, respiratory problems, irregular heartbeat, and extreme anorexia.

mescaline (peyote): A natural hallucinogen found in the peyote cactus, its only legal use is as a sacrament in the Native American Church of North America. The cactus is prepared and then softened in the mouth, and finally swallowed. It can also be manufactured chemically, powdered, and/or put into pills, smoked, or injected. Rarely, it can produce an amphetamine-like reaction.

HARMFUL EFFECTS: Users lose track of time and space, and may also hallucinate. Unfortunately, there is a scarcity of research on the physically harmful effects of this potent drug.

opiates: A class of drugs which includes heroin, codeine, morphine, hydrocodone and others. Opiates are compounds derived from opium, the milky residue of the opium poppy plant. Opium contains morphine and codeine among other substances. The naturally occurring morphine and codeine can be altered in the laboratory to produce "semi-synthetic" opiates, most notably heroin, hydrocodone, hydromorphone, and oxycodone, all of which can be abused.

HARMFUL EFFECTS: Sedation of reflexes and breathing, nausea and vomiting. To achieve the same effects over a long term, users must take increasingly large doses to overcome physical tolerance to the drug. Anyone using natural or synthetic opiates should be under the care of a doctor because of the high risk of overdose resulting in death. *See also* heroin.

pot: See marijuana.

psilocybin: An active hallucinogenic ingredient in some mushrooms and other fungi.

HARMFUL EFFECTS: Users may experience one or more of the following: separation anxiety, panic, hallucinations, feelings of heaviness, or, if the dosage is equivalent, most of the effects of LSD and mescaline.

psychedelic: Literally, "mind-manifesting." Of, relating to, or being drugs (such as LSD) capable of producing abnormal psychic effects (hallucinations) and sometimes psychic states resembling mental illness or artificial spiritual experience.

sanskara (Sanskrit): According to Meher Baba, sanskaras are "impressions" in the mind that are directly responsible for evolving consciousness as well as shaping experience and behavior. See the book *God Speaks* by Meher Baba for more information.

speed: See amphetamines.

In the United States of America, possessing, using, making, or selling amphetamines, ecstasy, hashish, heroin, LSD, marijuana, methamphetamines, and most prescription drugs without a prescription is illegal. There are federal and state laws that will punish offenders severely.

This glossary was reviewed and corrected by Allan Cohen, Rick Chapman, and Robert Dreyfuss. Some of the harmful effects were researched using norchemlab.com, theantidrug.com, and other resources. Some of the Hindi definitions were researched with Ameeta Vora using her Hindi–English dictionary.

NOTES

1. *Lord Meher*, vol. 2, p. 414 (ghazal translated by Adi K. Irani).

2. It is important to note that from 1925 (when he was thirty-one years old), until 1969, Meher Baba did not speak at all, although he had long stated that he would one day "break his Silence." Therefore, what he "said" and wrote, or any words attributed to him have come to us through one of the following communication methods:

   - He spoke the words before he started his silence on July 10, 1925, and someone wrote down what he actually said. The book *Mehera*, by Mehera J. Irani, shares many such occasions when Mehera heard Baba speak and even sing. Also, *Lord Meher* by Bhau Kalchuri shares many such occasions.

   - He wrote the words himself, in his own handwriting. This was very rare. The book *In God's Hand* by Meher Baba is a good example of this.

   - He dictated the words on an alphabet board, to be written up and published. The book *God Speaks*, by Meher Baba is a good example of this.

- He dictated specific points on a given theme, which were given to a writer chosen by him to expand the points. The expanded writing was brought back to Baba for his correction, clarification, and approval. Some of the material in *Discourses* by Meher Baba was written in this way.

- He gave written material authored by him to an individual author to be used in the preparation of a book or message, which was brought back to Baba for his correction, clarification, and approval before publication or distribution. The book *Listen, Humanity* by Meher Baba is a good example of this.

- He "dictated," using either the alphabet board or unique hand gestures, in the form of a discourse or a conversation with those present. This was then interpreted and recorded (or remembered) by someone present. It was Baba's habit to correct anyone who acted as his interpreter when he found any errors in the delivery of his communication. Baba went through great pains in his efforts to ensure that what was conveyed by an interpreter was true to his intended meaning. However, sometimes what was actually recorded of Baba's statements was written by a disciple in a personal diary or memoir, and remained unknown or unpublished until after Baba passed away in 1969. Many of the quotes and statements we have from Baba came to us in this way. The twenty volumes of Bhau Kalchuri's biography of Meher Baba, *Lord Meher,* are a good example of this.

3. *The Unstruck Music of Meher Baba,* by Maud Kennedy.

4. *Glimpses of the God-Man, Meher Baba*, by Bal Natu, vol. 1, p. 415.

5. *The Addictive Personality: Understanding the Addictive Process and Compulsive Behavior*, by Craig Nakken, p. 5.

6. *Messages for the New Humanity*, p. 18.

7. *God in a Pill?*, p. 3, and from *Lord Meher*, vol. 19, p. 6414. (letter from Baba to Richard Alpert).

8. *The Universal Message*, by Meher Baba.

9. *God in a Pill?*, p. 6.

10. This was written in a letter to Allan Y. Cohen on October 10, 1964, from Baba through his secretary Adi K. Irani. *Lord Meher*, vol. 19/20, p. 6283. See also *God in A Pill?* (© 1966 Sufism Reoriented, Inc., Walnut Creek, Calif.).

11. Letter is dated December 11, 1965. *Lord Meher*, vol. 19/20, p. 6411.

12. *The Glass Pearl*, ed. Naosherwan Anzar. Robert Dreyfuss read and approved *The Glass Pearl* version used in this manuscript. See also *Lord Meher*, vol. 19/20, pp. 6402-03.

13. November 1965, to Robert Dreyfuss at Meherazad. *Love Alone Prevails*, p. 638.

14. April 21, 1966. *Lord Meher*, vols. 19/20, pp. 6466-67.

15. One of the spiritual concepts that Meher Baba laid down as a foundation upon which he builds many other explanations is that of the subtle world, where an aspirant on the spiritual

path (one with subtle consciousness) can experience subtle planes of God's energy or power. According to Meher Baba, angels reside in the subtle world. For a detailed explanation of the subtle world, see *God Speaks*, by Meher Baba.

16. Meher Baba shed much light on the different types of Spiritual Masters, stating that the highest state of consciousness is that possessed by a God-realized Master (Perfect Master). This experience of God-realization is of Infinite Knowledge, Power, and Bliss, and it is very rare. For more information about Masters, Perfect Masters, and God-realization, see the books *God Speaks* and *Discourses*.

17. *Lord Meher*, vol. 19/20, p. 6469.

18. Mik Hamilton's visit was on March 7, 1966. *Lord Meher*, vol. 19/20, pp. 6425-33.

19. *The Messages, Discourses, and Sayings of Meher Baba Regarding Drugs*. Section on LSD.

20. *Lord Meher* vol. 19/20, p. 6474. Laurent gave Eruch a copy of the manuscript of this book in July 2001 at Meherazad, via Stephen Edelman. Laurent wrote a follow-up letter to Eruch on August 21, 2001, requesting his permission to include this story; however, Eruch passed away before responding to the letter.

21. *Lord Meher* vol. 19/20, pp. 6472-73. Don Stevens specifically requested (in an email to Laurent dated Friday, September 21, 2001) that he be referred to as "a follower of Meher Baba." Further, Don Stevens directly corrected the language quoted

(from *Lord Meher*) to clarify what he said to Meher Baba, so the subsequent notations describe these edits from him.

22. See the "*God in a Pill?* Revisited" chapter for a complete and sequential list of Baba's quotes on drugs from that publication.

23. Don Stevens clarified (in an email dated September 16, 2001) that he feels that a more accurate version of what he said to Baba used the word "much" in place of the word "more" in this sentence.

24. Don Stevens clarified (September 16, 2001): "...it could not possibly have been a tone, but rather a manner."

25. In messages sent to Laurent dated September 12 and 16, 2001.

26. *Lord Meher* vol. 19/20, p. 6473.

27. Dictated to Louis van Gasteren, transcribed from *Beyond Words* (1997), a video of his interview with Meher Baba, at Meherazad in 1967.

28. See note 2.

29. *The Messages, Discourses, and Sayings of Meher Baba Regarding Drugs*. Section on Legitimate Uses of Drugs.

30. *God in a Pill?*, p. 6-7.

31. *The Messages, Discourses, and Sayings of Meher Baba Regarding Drugs*. Section on LSD.

32. *The Awakener* 11:3, p. 4. Also, Robert Dreyfuss noted on this

manuscript that the first sentence of this quote was conveyed by Baba to him at Meherazad on November 17, 1965.

33. June 1966. *Lord Meher*, vol. 19/20, p. 6477.

34. *The Path of Love*, pp. 85-86. Also from *The Messages, Discourses, and Sayings of Meher Baba Regarding Drugs*, Section called "The 'Posing Saint' and the 'Opium Saint.'"

35. *The Messages, Discourses, and Sayings of Meher Baba Regarding Drugs*. Section called "The Messages of Avatar Meher Baba on Drugs."

36. *God in a Pill?*, p. 5.

37. *God in a Pill?*, p. 4.

38. *God in a Pill?*, pp. 5-6.

39. *Lord Meher*, vol. 19/20, p. 6470.

40. *God in a Pill?*, p. 2.

41. *God in a Pill?*, p. 3-4.

42. See note 9.

43. *Discourses* (7th ed.), pp. 277-78.

44. *The Messages, Discourses, and Sayings of Meher Baba Regarding Drugs*. Section on Liquor as a Drug.

45. *The Answer*, p. 26 (during the 1930s).

46. *The Messages, Discourses, and Sayings of Meher Baba Regarding Drugs*. Section on Wine.

47. Messages delivered during Andhra Tour (1954 booklet).

48. September 1929, in Ishfahan, Persia. *Lord Meher*, vol. 4, p. 1227.

49. *Lord Meher*, vol. 6, p. 1892.

50. March 1, 1953, Rishikesh. *Life Circulars*, p. 20. Also from *Life at Its Best*, pp. 67-68.

51. February 23, 1938. *Lord Meher*, vol. 7, p. 2267.

52. *Meher Gazette* 3:1, p. 22.

53. *Lord Meher*, vol. 3, p. 982.

54. *Questions Meher Baba Answered*, ed. K. K. Ramakrishnan, Part I, p. 25 (August 5, 1926). Also from *Meher Message* 1:11, pp. 6-7.

55 *Discourses* (7th ed.), p. 63.

56. *82 Family Letters*, by Mani S. Irani, p. 176.

57. *82 Family Letters*, p. 87.

58. *Is That So?*, p. 83.

59. *The Awakener* 19:2, p. 54.

60. *Life at Its Best*, p. 62-63.

61. *Treasures from the Meher Baba Journals*, p. 75.

62. *Discourses* (7th ed.), p. 299.

63. *The Everything and The Nothing*, p. 109.

64. *82 Family Letters*, p. 276.

65. *The Everything and The Nothing*, p. 72.

66. *Love Alone Prevails*, by Kitty Davy, p. 243.

67. *Discourses* (7th ed.), p. 157.

68. *Is That So?*, p. 83.

69. *God Speaks*, p. 178.

70. *The Path of Love*, p. 17.

71. *Meher Baba Calling*, p. 55.

72. *Life at Its Best*, pp. 26-27.

73. *Life at Its Best*, pp. 24-25.

74. "The Seven Realities" in *Discourses* (7th ed.), p. 2.

75. *Discourses* (7th ed.), p. 257.

76. *Love Alone Prevails*, pp. 683-84.

77. *Discourses* (7th ed.), p. 45.

78. *The Awakener*. 2: 4, p. 44.

79. *The Awakener* 14:3-4, p. 3.

80. *Discourses* (7th ed.), pp. 253-54.

81. *Discourses* (7th ed.), p. 254-55.

82. *Darshan Hours*, p. 62.

83. *The Path of Love*, p. 70.

84. *Glimpses*, vol. 1, p. 423.

85 It is a fine point to note that Meher Baba even cites these stages of the path as false experiences; however, because it is

the spiritual journey, these experiences serve to ignite in the seeker a greater longing for union with Beloved God, and therefore the experiences are spiritually helpful.

86. See note 16.

87. *Discourses* (7th ed.), pp. 8-9.

88. *The Everything and The Nothing*, p. 2.

89. *The Everything and The Nothing*, pp. 2-3.

90. *Lord Meher*, vol. 18, p. 5975.

91. *The Messages, Discourses, and Sayings of Meher Baba Regarding Drugs*. Section called "A Private Meeting with Meher Baba."

92. *Life at Its Best*, pp. 62-63.

93. *Meher Baba Calling*, p. 18.

94. Don Stevens continued his clarification (in an email message dated September 12 and 16, 2001,): "Although LSD use, as reported, had had no interest for me, I agreed to accept Murshida Duce's request and began the necessary reading and composition. In fact, Baba obviously intended this as a clever manner of getting me prepared for later tasks, as the editing work involved inevitably a good bit of thought and discussion, and it was at this time that I inherited four rebels of the 1960's vintage who changed my outlook entirely on the caliber of the people who were engaged in this wide and puzzling new quest for meaning in a technological age.

"It was as a result of trying to answer the questions of the

"Incidentally, the second incident when Baba and Eruch had to go into separate private conversation for some minutes before being able to give Don an approximation of what Baba was saying on an important topic, was Baba's insistence that I understand the great importance of certain words he gave out for public consumption. Eruch finally managed to explain in partially complete form, that Baba had tied to each of these very specially given words, something like an atom bomb of spiritual energy, and this spiritual energy would be absorbed by his devotees who worked with his words, even though they did not understand intellectually two words of what he was saying, and that this energy would be of the greatest value to them in their further spiritual ongoing.

"One needs to remember that Baba did not himself write letters but always gave them to Adi Sr. (Adi K. Irani) or Eruch or to Mani, and on rare occasions to others. Consequently Adi was, as I recall, frequently Baba's scribe from Baba to the three boys from Boston (Rick, Robert and Allan). Baba had Eruch describe the fine points of all this twice to me, and the important point to know is that Baba described very carefully that his very important words that had a spiritual atomic bomb attached to them were always given out first to a mandali and then written up by that mandali and then brought back to Baba and then Baba went through his minutely careful procedure of correcting word by word himself even to having the alphabet spelled out to spell especially key words. These are unique and our greatest heritage from Baba.

"I thought, as I skimmed this manuscript for a final time, of having the alphabet spelled out to spell especially key words. These are unique and our greatest heritage from Baba.

"I thought, as I skimmed this manuscript for a final time, of the actual editing of *God in a Pill?* those many years ago. A beautiful example of brain-washing came up. I had listened to so many of the young people in the group tell me that an LSD trip was no worse than a double martini cocktail that when I was drawing up the list of compounds forbidden by Baba, I had not included LSD among the forbidden. When one of the young members of the group read over the final draft he asked me, 'But don't you think you ought to include LSD?'

"I said 'No,' and he said, 'Don't you think you should ask Baba directly before publishing?' I said, 'OK, if he asked me to do it, I would.' So I sent off a telegram, I think it was, and promptly got back the reply that for certain Baba included LSD in the no no's. I was chagrined at the manner I had let myself be influenced by the propaganda I had been hearing for so long."

95. Baba said this to Robert Dreyfuss, November 17, 1965, as noted by Robert on the original manuscript of this book. Another version can be found in *Love Alone Prevails*, p. 638.

Acknowledgments

My Divine Beloved, Avatar Meher Baba, for just being, with me ... through all the years to this point in our wondrous adventure together! And thanks to all those with whom you have brought me into contact, to make this book possible:

My wife, Lilly, and daughter, Aspen, for being so supportive of this project (and bringing me food at the office so I could just work away). I love you both, more than you will ever know.

Sarah, my sister, for being there through thick and thin, in New York, Myrtle Beach, Georgia, and now Arizona.

Markar and Parkar for making me laugh when the world was not laughing.

Laura Smith for being so jazzed about working together on this for Baba. Laura, you have come such a long way and it is a privilege to work with you.

Andy Lesnik, Sheila Krynski, Ann Conlon, and everyone at Sheriar Foundation for believing in this project and shepherding it to final publication.

Allan Cohen for coming to Flagstaff and helping me find the confidence within to make progress on this drug work with Baba. Also, writing your foreword in Scorpio, so that I could offer this all to Baba before my new cycle. Allan, it is great to know you.

Rick Chapman for being so honest with me about my struggles. Rick, your real humility has been a great lesson to me. Also, all the time you put in with me on the phone and via email, to get the three forewords together! Also, for lending me the pillar of his words about Meher Baba.

Robert Dreyfuss for reviewing the draft,

agreeing to meet with me at his home, being so supportive of this process, and then surprising me with his foreword. It was a great pleasure to finally meet you.

Don Stevens for requesting the draft of the manuscript, reviewing the story about his discussion with Meher Baba regarding LSD, and providing much personal information via email which allowed me to more accurately report this story. Don, it has been one of my greatest pleasures to work with you in this way.

Mik Hamilton, for confirming the accuracy the *Lord Meher* description of your meeting with Beloved Baba, even though you and Ursula were not "hippies."

Alison Govi for sharing her responses to the manuscript, making so many incredibly valuable suggestions.

Dan Sanders for reviewing the manuscript twice, providing helpful input.

Tonya Crawford for your clear feedback, and

honesty. What you shared helped a lot.

Ms. Ameeta Vora for help with the translation of Hindi and Gujarati words used by Meher Baba, and teaching me how to say them properly...

And, thanks to whoever is actually reading this. It is only through you that the purpose of writing and publishing these words can be fulfilled.